The Three Pillars of Public Management
Secrets of Sustained Success

Written especially for the public sector, but applicable far beyond it, *The Three Pillars of Public Management* offers government managers insights that, for the first time, speak directly to their situation. Unlike other management books that promote fads and private-sector models or focus on politics, policy, and government-wide reforms, this book offers tangible suggestions to improve public service agencies.

Proving that public service excellence is not an oxymoron but an achievable reality, *The Three Pillars of Public Management* provides a framework for building and sustaining effective public service organizations based on the experiences of senior managers and a survey of top-performing public service organizations around the world. The authors find that success in serving the public rests on three pillars: the aim, or mission, of the organization; the character of the people and the institution; and execution — the way they get things done.

The Three Pillars of Public Management is an important resource for practitioners at all levels of the public service, from central agencies and top national departments to regional, state, or provincial governments and municipalities. With an easy-to-read style, inspiring examples, and a checklist of questions at the end of each chapter, the book is a valuable tool for improving the workplace.

OLE INGSTRUP is Commissioner of Corrections, Correctional Service of Canada. He is the co-author of *Our Story* in addition to numerous articles and reviews.

PAUL CROOKALL was senior advisor, Correctional Service of Canada, and is now a consultant in the private sector.

The Three Pillars
of Public Management

Secrets of Sustained Success

OLE INGSTRUP

and

PAUL CROOKALL

McGill-Queen's University Press
Montreal & Kingston • London • Ithaca

Legal deposit third quarter 1998
Bibliothèque nationale du Québec

Printed in Canada on acid-free paper

McGill-Queen's University Press acknowledges
the financial support of the Government of
Canada through the Book Publishing Industry
Development Program for its activities. We also
acknowledge the support of the Canada
Council for the Arts for our publishing program.

Canadian Cataloguing in Publication Data

Ingstrup, Ole
The three pillars of public management : secrets of
sustained success
Includes bibliographical references and index.
ISBN 0-7735-1813-4
1. Public administration.   I. Crookall, Paul Stanley, 1947-
II. Title.

JF1351.I52 1998   352.3   C98-900781-2

Typeset in 10½/13 Sabon by True to Type

*This book is dedicated to public servants around the world,
whose contributions make a difference to their society.
Their efforts, and their achievements, are our inspiration.*

Contents

CONTENTS

Acknowledgments

We are grateful to many people for their contributions to this book.

Harvey Schachter has made an enormous contribution. He did an outstanding job at follow-up interviews with respondents, and at making our work more readable. And he was fun to work with.

We are immensely grateful to the many public servants who took the time to respond to our survey, and interviews. The agencies are listed in the Appendix. An index provides page numbers on which specific people are mentioned. However, many more contributed whose names did not make it into these pages. Their contributions were, nonetheless, essential.

Many organizations, and individuals within those organizations, were generous and helpful in their support:

- The United Nations Division of Public Administration, Governance, and Finance, with Director Guido Bertucci and former Deputy Director A.T.R. Rahman, provided advice throughout the process. Many participants in the 1997 annual meeting of Experts in Public Administration and Finance reviewed and commented on an earlier draft and made valuable contributions.
- The International Institute of Administrative Science, with Don Hunn and David Brown, gave us an opportunity to present our findings to an international audience and benefit from discussion with them.
- The Commonwealth Association for Public Administration and Management, with Executive Director Art Stevenson and Gillian Mason, offered valuable advice and the opportunity to share our work with their members.

- The American Society for Public Administration, and Marc Holzer, invited us to present our work at their conference and provided welcome feedback.
- The Queen's University Skelton-Clark Fellowship program and many colleagues there, where the survey phase of this work was conducted. The Skelton-Clark Fellows, Professor Gordon Cassidy, the Executive Development Program faculty and participants.
- The Treasury Board Secretariat and the Public Service Commission for their support from the beginning of this work.
- The Canadian Centre for Management Development, where the early development was supported, and Ralph Heintzman and Brian Marson for their support and counsel.
- The Correctional Service of Canada for its support during the writing of the book.
- The Office of the Clerk of the Privy Council, and Jocelyne Bourgon, for their wonderful assistance in connecting with agencies and governments around the world, and opening doors.

Many individuals have generously given of their time to help us improve the text through their reviews and comments, including Lou Auerback, Bruce Avolio, Maria Barrados, Julian Barling, Carol Beattie, Sandford Borons, Tim Crookall, Robert Dandurand, Stewart Fyfe, Willie Gibbs, Eva Kmiecic, Michel Lamoureux, Peter Larson, Claire Lord, Jim McDavid, Brendan Reynolds, Alec Ross, Gloria Saccon, Bill Staubi, The Yukon Territory's meeting of Deputy Ministers, and many others.

We are also grateful to the staff at McGill-Queen's University Press, and their reviewers, for their assistance and their understanding in dealing with us.

One of the most precious things we have gained from researching and writing this book is the friendship and inspiration of those we have worked with and gotten to know better.

Most of all, we appreciate the work carried out by the hidden heroes who work in the agencies we studied, who have learned the secrets of sustained success and practice them daily in the service of their countries.

In sharing their stories, and their words, we have two requests of the reader. We offer this book as our understanding of what was told to us by many people. We recognize that we cannot pass along what another person told us, or wrote, or meant; we can only pass along what we heard, or read, or understood. We recognize that, over time, the people and the situations we have reported on may change, and that we may have not gotten it down precisely as our sources intended. For our readers, we request that you accept any errors or embarrassments as our own, not those of the contributors.

Our second request is to treat this book in the manner that Rupert Ross suggests in *Return to the Teachings*: "Read what follows in the same way you would pick up a strangely shaped piece of driftwood. Hold it for a while in your hands, glance over its knots and swirls and shadows and see if it 'says' anything to you. If it does, you are free to use it as you will. If it does not, leave it where you found it, just in case it is capable of touching the next unique human beings who come along. What means little to you may mean much to them – and vice versa – and that in itself is cause for celebration."

In acknowledgment of the support from the Government of Canada for this research, we have arranged for all royalties to be sent to the Government of Canada.

The Three Pillars of Public Management

CHAPTER 1

Learning from the Best

Sometimes public servants toil in obscurity. Sometimes they work in a fishbowl. Either way, it's rare that their expertise is widely celebrated. But when the U.S. Veterans Benefits Administration regional office in Muskogee, Oklahoma, won a President's Quality Award for high standards of customer service and quality, the *Muskogee Daily Phoenix* saluted the achievement with an editorial.

"We've heard it before. Government is unresponsive. Government is irresponsible. Government is inefficient," the editor began. "But as always, there is another side to the story. For example, the national average on processing a widow's benefits claim is 76 days. In Muskogee, provided the applicant has the proper paperwork in hand, a widow's claim can be processed in a single day."

Leaders determined to improve quality and service trusted their employees enough to transfer decision-making to front-line workers in self-directed teams. "The employees at the Muskogee VA office are to be congratulated for doing their jobs so well – and for showing that the job can be well done," the editorial concluded.

When Egyptians first traveled the Internet information highway, a public agency charged with improving the information and decision-making capacity of the government bureaucracy led the way. Some people might expect a body with the title Cabinet Information and Decision Support Center to be a lumbering centralized agency, not a swift-and-savvy crew. But the center has served as a catalyst for establishing a flourishing computer industry in Egypt that will be able to meet the demands of government, business and the public.

For several years, the center was the country's main Internet access provider, until it spun the work off to private firms it had nurtured. When *Computer World*[1] magazine published a special issue on the Global 100 – the organizations around the world using information technology most effectively – this arm of the Egyptian public service was honored alongside the best of the international private sector.

In Denmark, the National Board of Industrial Injuries rules on claims by injured workers against insurance agencies. After a century of providing excellent service, it was starting to feel its age. Decisions had become too complicated and took too long to reach. The agency was remodeled, with more freedom granted to innovate as long as it meets the performance outcomes in an annual agreement signed with its two overseeing ministries. As an incentive, any profit the board garners from streamlined operations can be distributed as incentive pay to the employees.

The board now routinely surpasses its service standards, with appropriate financial rewards and without sacrificing Scandinavian-style workplace features like flexible hours, special care days for parents, and a masseuse for employees' aching muscles. "After 100 years, an organization starts to live its own life," says Marianne Hvolris, head of the board's information technology department. "The organization becomes a goal in itself rather than the customer. We had to change from a traditional bureaucratic attitude to a service attitude."

THE HIDDEN HEROES

Those three agencies are vastly different organizations that operate in very distinct cultures and government settings.* But they share one important feature: each is a well-performing government organization. In an era when the gladiators of private enterprise draw the glory, little attention is paid to the hidden heroes of public service. The popular books on management analyse, re-analyse, and

---

* Unless clearly indicated in this book, we will use the words agency, department, and organization as synonyms for the work units we studied.

re-analyse again a small number of top American corporations, seeking universal managerial truths. Often ignored are the many people who work for government – at the national, regional, and local level, as well as in educational institutions, hospitals, and utilities.

They aren't all second-class managers. Nonetheless, an inferiority complex has been bred in public service managers by their absence from most popular management books and from the rhetoric of the times. It's as if only those other managers in the private sector struggle with change and only those other managers in the private sector achieve excellence. In contrast to that perception, however, noted management professor Henry Mintzberg, who consults and teaches in both sectors, has observed: "Many of the most intelligent, articulate and effective managers I have met work for government."

This book is intended for those managers, and for anyone interested in effective public service. It's based on a unique international study of well-performing public organizations, which uncovered nine common features that appear to be essential to good performance. In this chapter we'll summarize the main lessons derived from our study. In the chapters following, we'll focus on one of those nine key areas, offering vivid examples from the frontlines of some well-performing organizations and our own thoughts as researchers and practitioners.

Government, with its multiple bottom lines and range of stakeholders, is as formidable an arena for managers as the private sector – perhaps even more challenging. An effective public service is essential to the economic, social, and political health of every country. A well-developed and effective public sector is, ironically, one of the prerequisites for a well-developed and effective private sector. An effective public sector is now an essential factor in global competitiveness.

Not every public service meets those challenges. Nevertheless, under difficult conditions, many public organizations around the globe routinely deliver high-quality service. Those well-performing organizations are committed to their mandates and to the citizens they serve. They meet or exceed their stakeholders' expectations – and have been doing so for a long time. They contribute significantly to their country's fiscal and social well being.

FOUR COMPETING DEMANDS

Today's public servants face a daunting task. They labor within complex policy frameworks and under intense economic, social, technological, and competitive pressures. They encounter increasing, and often conflicting, demands from citizens, interest groups, and politicians.

Those demands fall into four broad areas. The first is fiscal pressure, which has forced a review of public services and their delivery methods. Many government departments are being cut, merged, or eliminated. Economy and efficiency ride high on the political agenda. Even jurisdictions with balanced budgets pay rigorous attention to expenses because society today places a high priority on cost-effective government.

The second major pressure is widespread public concern about the speed, quality, and appropriateness of government services. Clearly, citizens believe that the services delivered don't match what is needed. A recent multi-nation survey revealed that even in the top-rated country, Canada, only 51 per cent of respondents were satisfied with their public service – a distressingly feeble result for the leading country, and worse for the laggards.[2]

A related problem is that the public's expectations for government services are changing in ways that are not always clearly defined or communicated. The public seems to sense what is inadequate, yet it is often hard-pressed to define what "good service" actually means. In some countries in North America and Europe, the pressure is for less government and better service at lower cost. In other countries, such as South Africa and the former communist block, they want to change the very fabric of their society, and that, in turn, increases government intervention.

The third major pressure is that public servants increasingly find themselves operating in a fishbowl. The public has easy access to all corners of the public service, media scrutiny is harsh, and access-to-information laws abound. That is only reasonable, of course, but a byproduct of this new fishbowl era is that everyone – business leaders, politicians, interest groups, individuals, and media pundits – feels free to offer helpful, and sometimes not-so-helpful, advice about how to manage the public service. Each is an instant expert, without the necessary background knowledge.

Finally, the pace of change in our globalized, plugged-in CNN world affects the public sector, imposing powerful pressure for quick change on a system built for stability. Everybody expects instant solutions to non-instant problems.

FEW SOLID THEORIES

Remarkably little research and few solid theories exist on how to achieve excellence in public management. Certainly, as a society, we have not forged an agreement on how to build a public service that performs well over the long term. Various explanations have been offered and solutions prescribed, but we still have no clearly defined model of an effective public service and our definition of the public management profession remains sketchy at best. Much of the focus, as well, has been on overall political and structural reform rather than the specific management techniques required for success within the individual units of the public service.

RESEARCH APPROACH

As senior managers in the public service, we have worked in, studied, and consulted with a variety of public agencies on four continents, and have associated with public sector colleagues from all over the world. We've seen some of the best organizations imaginable, and some of the worst. As a result of that experience, we identified key areas that we thought could be linked to managerial success. To explore them further, we sent questionnaires to agencies that were identified as well-performing – and had been so for at least five years if not, preferably, a decade or longer. The questions were highly open-ended and, as an additional safeguard, specifically asked if we had missed any critical factors in our probing.

In the end, we received impressively detailed, thoughtful responses from 40 agencies in 14 countries. We heard from high-profile police, social services, and health care departments; little-known agencies such as armaments research and cabinet support; large or geographically dispersed departments of foreign affairs, agriculture, and transport; as well as small single-site groups, such as mapping. Responses ranged from G-7 countries to small island nations. We followed up with interviews in many of the agencies. Finally, we consulted extensively with public sector leaders, practitioners, and academics.

Respondent Countries

Australia	Canada	Costa Rica	Denmark	Egypt
Lebanon	Malta	Mexico	New Zealand	Norway
Philippines	Singapore	Switzerland	United States	

THE THREE PILLARS

The responses suggest that three pillars support success in well-per-forming agencies:

1 Aim: The top agencies know clearly the direction they are headed in. Their mission is deeply ingrained in the daily actions and long-term planning of the organization rather than simply hanging on the wall in the reception area. A long-time leader often exemplifies the mission and everyone is held accountable to it.

2 Character: These agencies have a strong sense of who they are and what is important. That organizational character, fueled by a high degree of trust, is communicated internally and external-ly through principle-centred activities. The people in the agency, and the agencies themselves, exude a sense of integrity, trust, caring, openness and, crucially, a desire to learn.

3 Execution: These organizations get things done, achieving their aim and demonstrating their character through the use of a broad array of management tools. They innovate in an era of never-ending change, realizing that the tools and techniques they employ are a means to an end, not ends in themselves. Teamwork is an essential element: they know how to roll up their sleeves, work together, and implement effectively.

The three pillars of public management are mutually supportive. The well-performing organizations can execute effectively because they know the mission and have character. Their character is rein-forced through their focus on a noble mission and successful imple-mentation. Their aim is an outgrowth of their character, and top-flight execution helps to achieve the mission.

The three pillars are composed of nine clearly delineated man-agement elements. Leaders of well-performing organizations pay attention to all nine elements – not just to six or seven or eight, but to all nine. The elements fall symmetrically into our three pillars, making it easy to remember them:

The Three Pillars

Aim	Character	Execution
Mission	People	Management Tools
Leadership	Communication	Teamwork
Accountability	Trust	Change Management

None of these attributes will come as a surprise to experienced managers. Each has been discussed at length in the management literature. But again we stress: our research shows that these elements are common to all well-performing public organizations. They are also easy to grasp – elements of organizational life that each of us can influence from whatever our perch in public management. They therefore serve as a starting point for those intent on improvement.

Aim

Mission It has become routine for organizations to prepare mission statements. But in top-performing organizations, mission statements are more than routine. They are a constant presence in operations, entrenched in the minds and daily activity of the organization.

Leadership We thought that culture, geography, diversity of service, and local politics would lead to specific leadership activities that worked well in one situation but would be inappropriate in another. In the end we found examples of that, but far fewer than we expected. Instead, certain themes or principles kept recurring. They included the need for listening, involving, and delegating; commitment to employees; and consistency between the leadership style and the mission.

Consistency was also demanded from the organization's leaders. The organizations don't tolerate an Attila the Hun in one office and a Mother Teresa next door. Word and deed must also be in harmony: leaders of well-performing organizations must walk the talk.

Leadership also extends beyond the organization itself to influencing fellow agencies, the public, and even the private sector, as exemplified by the Norwegian Petroleum Directorate's instrumental role in bringing total quality practices to the oil industry operating on their coast.

Finally, leaders take the long view, knowing the organization and its staff will exist for a long time and therefore wanting to get things right. Indeed, our findings echoed the research in *Built To Last*,[3] an examination of visionary companies in the private sector. Although it is increasingly common for heads of public service departments to have short tenure, many of ours have been around for a long time and most came up through their own organization. For younger agencies, the founder was often still active. The Mexican National Institute of Nutrition, a hospital for internal medicine, has only had four directors in its 50 years. The founder, Dr Salvador Zubirán, remains, at age 98, an inspiring presence through his attendance at ceremonies.

Accountability   At its core, accountability involves agencies and individuals explaining what they are doing. They tell their stories – and live with the consequences. Those consequences should be both good and bad. Traditionally, accountability systems have focused on the bad. In the well-performing organizations, we found structures that directly linked mission and accountability, with results rather than activities being measured. Deviations were dealt with. Successes were celebrated, internally and externally. Incentives were more common than we expected, ranging from certificates of achievements, to days off, to free dinners, to performance-based pay.

Together, mission, mission-focused accountability, and mission-focused leadership provide a powerful sense of direction. Successful organizations take aim at noble goals. They have setbacks – daily small ones and occasional big ones. But with leadership, mission, and accountability synchronized, they know when they are veering off course and readjust before they become lost. They operate within an overall direction that can be seen, literally, stretching back a century or more in many cases and at the same time stretching forward into the future to make a contribution to their society.

Character

People The phrase "people are our most important resource" has become a tired, overworked cliché. Our respondents used that cliché, but were quick to follow up with documentation on what they actually accomplished – from developing a family-friendly workplace, to training and development, to delegation.

The organizations are sensitive to the concerns of their employees and display it through a variety of techniques, from surveys to open door policies. At Canada's National Library, management listened, ten years ago, through a staff attitude survey. They listened further with follow-up focus groups on specific issues. They kept listening through ongoing working groups drawn from cross-sections of the staff. They responded with improvements in staff development, incentives, awards, and innovation. A decade later, they are still listening – and following up.

Communication From e-mail to a leisurely tea with the boss, these organizations have multiple channels of communication. Attention is paid to three main audiences – employees, clients, and partners – with each agency spending time thinking about their communication needs and the appropriate solutions. Canada's National Library even has a checklist guideline for communications in frequently occurring situations, and an annual communications plan.

These well-performing organizations have also moved out of their traditional hierarchical or vertical structures (silos), to network with an array of partners. As society has become increasingly complicated, fewer and fewer issues can be resolved by one agency. Most issues are now horizontal. Nova Scotia Fisheries, in one of Canada's smallest provinces, has membership on over 100 inter-agency and industry committees.

Trust The well-performing organizations call trust everything from the glue that holds them together to the lubricant that facilitates their operations. Whatever the proper metaphor, it's clear that trust is central to effective operations. To thrive, individuals must be able to trust the organization and their colleagues within the organization. Trust reduces stress and fear. It is a prerequisite for honesty and openness, which in turn are prerequisites for organizational learning. Well-performing organizations are classic learning organizations.

Our well-performing agencies try to avoid the traditional "Gotcha!" reflex to errors. This new spirit was exemplified by the Northwest Territories Workers' Compensation Board: "All results are seen in a positive light. Good results are celebrated, unsatisfactory results are used to sort out mistakes and shift direction." These organizations learn.

Execution

Management Tools   Well-performing agencies don't subscribe to any one management guru or tool. They also don't succumb to the flavor-of-the-month in management approaches. They constantly seek to improve their tools, by assessing what is available and how it fits with their agency and its needs. Consistency is important, as they apply available techniques from a well-stocked tool box that seem appropriate for specific management tasks.

Teamwork   More and more public service organizations are employing teams for a wide range of purposes. Each agency in the survey expressed support for teams and an intention to increase their usage. Two agencies had even moved to a full self-managed team approach. More importantly, all the agencies were imbued with a sense of teamwork, a collegial win-win approach to their jobs, whether or not a "team" was actually working on the project.

The atmosphere of trust fosters teamwork. We thought some major cultural differences would arise between the competitive North American culture and other, more instinctively supportive cultures. We did find a difference in style: North American and European teams tended to be more "business-like," while other cultures had more "family-like" teams. But all tackled similar issues.

Change Management   Change is ever-present and unending. Pierre Gravel, then Revenue Canada's deputy minister, put it well: "National governments simply have no choice but to respond and to adapt, and then, to respond and adapt again. Change can no longer be managed as a singular event ... it is unlikely that we will have the luxury of seeing through [the present change] before it is overtaken by the next wave of change." Indeed, all governments face such challenges: new legislation, reduced budgets, more demands, suddenly emerging technology, changing clientele. At the extreme, the administration of Metropolitan Toronto – a widely admired body that delivered major services in a city that has been consistently ranked as one of the top ten cities in the world to live in – has been abolished since our survey, forcibly merged with several other adjacent cities. (And Gravel has experienced personal job change, moving on to another position in the interval between our research and publication.)

Change has become a way of life. Organizations can't "ride out the storm." Our respondents tackle change head-on, leading it, treating it as an ally rather than an opponent. At the same time, they are acutely aware that change has a negative impact on employees. They try to help the employees absorb the impact and readjust.

ADDING SOCRATES

We believe it's vital to embed our three pillars in a special foundation: a questioning, Socratic approach. Socrates, in his bare feet and toga, seems an odd leader for public managers to emulate. But some of his character traits would be surprisingly fresh today. He was called the wisest man in Greece and said that he accepted that mantle only because his wisdom came from knowing his own ignorance. He was not just a philosopher. He was a decorated war hero, who on return to civilian life sought to improve government and the public service. He educated youth, not a bad feature for today's mentoring leader. And he had integrity, choosing to obey the rule of law and take the poisonous hemlock rather than escape into exile.

The feature of Socrates we wish to emphasize, however, is that he sought truth by asking questions, often highly provocative and even embarrassing questions that revealed unexpected truths to him and those he engaged in dialogue. The method worked then and it works today. It's the approach on which we based our survey – we asked a dozen critical questions and learned from the results. Our survey wasn't a formal Socratic dialogue, of course, and we're not suggesting such rigor in the workplace. But a questioning style works well in the day-to-day labors of public managers. Good managers realize their wisdom comes from knowing their own ignorance and therefore asking a lot of questions.

It's also a style we have brought to this book. It would be easy to claim we have found some instant formula for managerial success: nine miracle ingredients that form three crucial pillars. Life isn't that simple, however. Instead, we believe our findings have to be viewed as a starting point for explorations rather than as an end point. Our nine attributes are not a checklist of guaranteed solutions but rather a checklist of important questions that leaders of well-performing institutions seem to ask – and that we feel others would be wise to apply to their own agencies.

Saying an organization needs a mission, for example, only starts the process. What type of mission? How do you develop it? How do you instill it in the staff so that they take it to heart? How do you tie it to accountability? How do you update it? In that vein, we conclude each chapter with a section called Explorations: a set of questions – meant for you to add to – that might lead your agency towards improved performance.

STEAK NOT SIZZLE

It is important to recognize that our framework presupposes a political, social, and economic environment in which public servants can flourish. As Robert Doodoo, head of Ghana's Civil Service, told us when we met at the United Nations with representatives of developing countries: "You can talk of the three pillars but the political environment is crucial. If the political environment is no good – a coup every two years – the public service is unstable, nothing is sustained, and it's two steps backward for every step forward." But we were heartened that he and others at that meeting shared our belief that the model and the approach provide guidance to and support for those seeking a more stable, democratic society.

Public service organizations face an increasingly stormy climate in which to provide excellent service, yet some continue to do so. This book, based on the experience of senior public servants and a world-wide survey of successful public service agencies, provides a framework for improving public service organizations. We believe we have captured the essential features of well-performing organizations, the steak (or in vegetarian cuisine the soybean) rather than the sizzle.

Our structure is clearcut: three pillars, each with three essential elements. And it's all propelled by a Socratic questioning of our organizations and ourselves. The three pillars – Aim, Character, and Execution – combine with our Socratic foundation to form a handy acronym, ACES, that will help managers remember the ideas. The model allows for diversity, is achievable, and has proven successful for the well-performing organizations in our sample. Public servants can now learn from excellence in their own field.

Three Pillars of Public Management

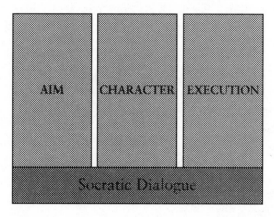

CAPSULES

- In an era when the gladiators of private enterprise draw the glory, little attention is paid to the hidden heroes of public service who also manage to achieve excellence.
- Government, with its multiple bottom lines and range of stakeholders, is as challenging an arena to manage in as the private sector – perhaps even more challenging.
- Public servants face four compelling demands: fiscal pressure, public concern about the quality of services, a fishbowl atmosphere, and unrelenting change.
- We found Three Pillars of Public Management: Aim, Character, and Execution.
- Nine attributes are associated with those well-performing organizations, three with each pillar.
- Aim involves Mission, Leadership, and Accountability.
- Character involves People, Communication, and Trust.

- Execution involves Management Tools, Teamwork, and Change Management.
- Well-performing organizations support those pillars with a questioning, Socratic style.
- We believe we have captured the essential features of well-performing organizations, the steak or soybean rather than the sizzle.
- The three pillars of <u>A</u>im, <u>C</u>haracter, and <u>E</u>xecution combine with our <u>S</u>ocratic approach to form the acronym ACES, an easy way to remember the essentials of effective, well-performing public service agencies. ACES is a powerful antidote for combating poor performance.

EXPLORATIONS

Does your organization perform well?

What are its best features?

Which of the nine elements are weak or need improving in your organization?

Is there a will to improve?

Might the Socratic method and the ideas in this book contribute to your efforts?

What might be some ways to begin the dialogue leading to change?

Do the poorly performing public service organizations you know have aim, character, and execution?

Do the well performing public service organizations you know have aim, character, and execution embedded in a questioning dialogue?

Who do you talk with about good public management? What questions do you ask?

CHAPTER 2

Studying The Best

In 1988 Canada's auditor-general took an unusual detour in his annual report to Parliament. Normally the document is an extensive catalogue of everything that's gone wrong in the public service. But in that year's publication, the auditor-general added a chapter on what had gone right.

In it, he examined eight government organizations that were considered to be top performers and sought to identify the features that contributed to their high accomplishment. The chapter, written by Otto Brodtrick,[1] was one of the first efforts to investigate the secrets of success for well-performing public service organizations and is a progenitor of our own study.

The well-performing organizations were suggested by those in a position to know in such central operations as the Office of the Comptroller-General and the Treasury Board Secretariat. They identified three government departments, one board, two Crown corporations, a special office created to coordinate the 1988 Calgary Winter Olympics, and, finally, a joint project between two government agencies. Brodtrick wrote:

When we considered our findings, we reached an overall conclusion: the well-performing organizations have been able to move 'beyond bureaucracy.' One may say that they have moved from being public bureaucracies to being public enterprises, if we construe the term bureaucracy to mean red tape and unresponsiveness and if we characterize public enterprise by innovation, responsiveness and productivity.

Bureaucracies tend to make the activities routine and predictable, basing their operations on standardized rules. They also tend to set up controls that seek to ensure compliance with these rules. However, the demands of customers frequently change, requiring the very flexibility and innovation that has been standardized out of the bureaucracy's operations. Because of the conflict, there tends to be a gap of unresponsiveness between the bureaucracy and the people it serves. Furthermore, a bureaucracy tends to frustrate efforts by its own staff to break out of this framework of inertia. It tends to meet challenges to its own rules by tightening up. Typically, the insight that rigidity may be counterproductive does not occur to it.

Nowadays that observation wouldn't draw as much attention. But a decade ago Brodtrick was charting the first stirrings of what has been dubbed "the new public management." From the study he delineated five attributes of well-performing public organizations that were absent from or much reduced in poorly performing public organizations:[2]

1   Emphasis on people: In well-performing organizations, people are challenged, encouraged, and developed. They are given power to act and to use their judgment. The prevailing belief is that high performance is a product of people who care rather than systems that constrain. Staff do not preoccupy themselves with the risk of failure but are confident they can tackle virtually any challenge.
2   Participative Leadership: Leadership in the organization is not authoritarian or coercive but participative whenever possible. The leaders envision an ideal organization, define purpose and goals, then articulate these and foster commitment. Staff communicate easily. They feel comfortable consulting their peers as well as those above and below them. Although formal levels exist for administrative purposes, no boundaries inhibit collaboration in achieving goals.
3   Innovative work styles: Staff learn from their actions and seek to solve problems creatively. They maintain strong monitoring, feedback, and control systems as useful tools. They are self-reliant, rather than dependent on control from an outside authority.
4   Strong client orientation: These organizations focus firmly on their clients, deriving satisfaction from serving the client rather than the bureaucracy. Alignment of values and purpose exists between the well-performing organizations and their political and central agency masters, with a view to strong performance and high achievement.
5   A mindset that seeks optimum performance: people hold values that drive them to always seek improvement in organizational performance.

When conditions change, they adjust their methods, not their values. Because of this mindset – probably the most important attribute of the five, Brodtrick argued – the organizations perform well even in a changing environment. Their operating philosophy seems to be: "The world is messy. Hence, to manage well, we need to develop managers who can perform productively in work environments that are messy, uncertain, and changing. This makes it possible to have high-performing organizations.

If you walk into any large bookstore and look for books on public sector management, you won't find Brodtrick's study, despite its obvious value. That's not unexpected since it was a slice of an internal Canadian government report with another main purpose. But what's more significant is that you probably won't find many other books on the subject either. If you talk to the staff, they will generally steer you toward the politics section, where you might uncover half a dozen works on public management sprinkled among those on government and policy-making.

In most countries, 10 to 20 per cent of the work force is in the public service and the outcome of their work is critical to the success of the private sector. Given that, it's surprising that so little is written on public management, that so much of what is written is opinion-based rather than research-based. Indeed, one of the few authors to be honest about this, Charles Goodsell, subtitled his book "a personal polemic."[3]

The books that are written tend to cover three overlapping areas. One deals with the role of the state: what should the business of government be? Should government be interventionist or laissez-faire, expanding or shrinking, looking after each citizen from cradle to grave, or simply creating a level playing field for the private sector? British Prime Minister Thatcher promised to "roll back the frontiers of the state" in 1979. That approach is driven in part by the fiscal imperatives noted in chapter 1, but also by a philosophy tracing back to Thomas Paine and Henry David Thoreau who held "that government is best that governs least."

A second area of study grapples with the machinery of government, which is a subset of politics. Should there be one or two legislative assemblies? How should powers be divided between national and local governments? Should the public service be controlled by several strong central agencies or should ministers contract with private-sector-like chief executive officers of separate, business-like agencies? How should the auditor general or the General Accounting Office ensure that the individual departments are operating well, and honestly?

The third, and least-studied, area is the management of public service organizations. Given that a certain role has been defined for the state, and certain machinery of government legislated, how does the individual public service manager carry out his or her work productively? In effect, the first two streams focus more on what is to be *done to* the departments while the third is more interested in what is to be *done by* the departments.

Most public servants are concerned with all three fields of study. They must be mindful of the role of government and the machinery of government. But the most important area for them – which preoccupies them daily – is how to manage within this special environment. It's also the area on which most public servants can have some impact. It's hard for them to alter the role of the state or the machinery of government. But every public servant can, at least to some degree, improve the quality of services offered at his or her workplace.

This book offers assistance in that effort. In this chapter, we will review the literature in the third area, public management writing, placing our own study in context. Readers who are already familiar with these writings, or who want to plunge immediately into the results of our study, can skip this chapter or come back to it later without any loss of continuity.

OSBORNE AND GAEBLER REINVENT GOVERNMENT

In the bookstore we conjured up earlier, the one book you're most likely to find is David Osborne and Ted Gaebler's best seller, *Reinventing Government*,[4] the most popular public sector management book. The authors didn't set out to catalogue a wide range of well-performing organizations but instead wanted to draw attention to a new entrepreneurial spirit they feel is transforming the public sector. While the examples in that book are impressive and most of the organizations they cite no doubt perform ably, if not superbly, the book has a messianic and somewhat political flavor.

In particular, the authors push for government to pull back – steer rather than row – and allow more of its functions to be carried out by other entities, notably the private sector. The public sector is also expected to act more like the private sector in its own activities. That thrust appears to be rooted in the first category of public management books, those devoted to the role of government.

But they go on to give advice and practical examples that are useful to public service managers trying to get their job done better, summarized in the box below.

Reinventing Government: The Ten Point Program

1 Steer rather than row: government must act as a catalyst. Delivering services is rowing and government is not very good at rowing. Instead, it must steer others who can better deliver services.

2 Empower rather than serve: governments can be most effective by helping people and communities to help themselves.

3 Inject competition into service delivery: the issue for service delivery is not public vs private but competition vs monopoly. The public is best served when several organizations – perhaps some from government and some from the private sector – compete against each other in service delivery.

4 Transform rule-driven organizations into mission-driven organizations: government authorities must set goals and let public managers figure out the best means of attaining those objectives.

5 Fund outcomes, not inputs: public-sector managers must focus on the results of their work, using performance standards and other measurements.

6 Meet the needs of the customer, not the bureaucracy: government must make its customers feel valued. Public-sector managers must operate with the same zeal as business executives who know their sales and profits depend on customers.

7 Earn rather than spend: government must adjust to the tax revolt by innovatively finding new, non-tax revenue sources.

8 Prevention rather than cure: government must anticipate problems and prevent them from occurring or at least limit their impact.

9 Move from hierarchy to participation and teamwork: entrepreneurial leaders must decentralize, shifting many decisions to the

> periphery – into the hands of customers, communities, and
> non-governmental organizations or, within their own units, to
> employees in more-flattened workplaces.
> 10 Leverage change through the market: governments must use
> market mechanisms to achieve their goal, rather than instinc-
> tively reacting to problems by devising new administrative pro-
> grams.

Reinventing Government was itself partially reinvented by
Osborne and a new co-author, Peter Plastrik, in *Banishing Bureaucracy*.[5] This time five strategies were presented to help managers
implement the reinventing model: creating clarity of purpose; creating consequences for performance; putting the customer in the
driver's seat; shifting control away from the top and center; and creating an entrepreneurial culture.

Interestingly, they found at the government-wide level what we
found at the individual agency level: countries are acting in remarkably similar ways in trying to improve their public management.
Unlike each of our agencies, however, whose aim is crystal clear and
rock solid, Osborne and Plastrik found "most reinventors are still
operating without a road map." Perhaps that is because, as
Osborne and Plastrik confess, "*Reinventing Government* was not
designed to help readers figure out how to proceed. It described the
characteristics of entrepreneurial governments – how they act and
what they do – but it did not discuss how to create them."

Reinventing Government was one of the bases for the National
Performance Review, the Clinton government's approach to public
sector reform spearheaded by Vice President Al Gore. Yet Gore
reports it was public servants themselves who made the difference.
"Behind virtually every bit of our successful downsizing and stream-
lining are the ideas and the enthusiasm of federal workers. More
than anyone, they have the know-how and the desire to make government cost less."[6]

Osborne, Plastrik, and Gaebler's advice might work well in the
United States but would have less applicability in other parts of the
world, since their belief that government must pull back can't be
universally applied. In many countries, for example, providing jobs
is considered a vital public sector function. As well, each country is
at a different stage of its life cycle and can have strikingly different

requirements of government. In Canada's early days, the federal government built a railway to bind the nation together. Today that service and the similar national airline have been essentially taken out of government's hands. Yet in emerging nations today, governments will have to play the central role in building such infrastructure. If some developing nations were to apply Osborne and Gaebler's ideas, their country might draw to a grinding, absolute halt.

It's also questionable whether a significant performance differential exists between private and public, as some reformers claim. We can find good public-sector and bad public-sector organizations, just as we can find good and bad private-sector businesses. In North America, hundreds of thousands of companies collapse into bankruptcy each year. The American savings and loan industry imploded and citizens who had invested were rescued by the government. The Bre-X mining fiasco saw millions of dollars fleeced from unsuspecting North American investors who bought visions of gold in Indonesia's Busang region. Presumably those companies are not part of the private sector that the public service is supposed to emulate.

Finally, Osborne and Gaebler's central prescription of steering rather than rowing is also undercut by the fact most of the government operations they chronicled are highly adept at rowing. The authors didn't analyse policy units. They looked primarily at municipal and county organizations that are all busily rowing. It would be difficult to apply their findings to the diplomats in a foreign affairs ministry or to Canadian officials overseeing the highly sensitive unity file in the aftermath of the 1995 referendum in which Quebeckers nearly voted to separate. Indeed, it's ironic that they come to the conclusion that government should steer and not row on the basis of wonderful examples of government rowing well.

That reflects a common bias. The daily news is replete with examples and accounts of poor public service. A person who considers that list of mistakes and foul-ups could be forgiven for concluding the public service is in a mess and desperately needs drastic surgery. Russell Mills, publisher of the *Ottawa Citizen*,[7] puts this in some perspective, however, by advising that the media is in the business of reporting on what people talk about – what they are interested in.

People don't talk about the thousands of airplanes that land safely every day, and how much safer flying is than driving. They talk about their fear of flying and the crashes. Similarly, the public does not talk about the thousands of public employees who take a sandwich to work. But they do talk about the one public servant who quaffs champagne and munches caviar paid for by a government expense account.

ECHOING BRODTRICK

The fact that some public service organizations perform poorly does not prove that there are no organizations that perform well.

Several other authors on public service management have echoed elements of Brodtrick's work and added related concepts. Steven Cohen, in *The Effective Public Manager*,[8] noted that organizations should seek to shape the future rather than be shaped by events. James McDavid and Brian Marson, in *The Well-Performing Government Organization*,[9] mentioned that such organizations must reduce barriers and constraints, earn employees' commitment, have effective leadership, provide customer service, and gain central agency and political support. Robert Denhardt, in *The Pursuit of Significance*,[10] stressed that they should demonstrate their commitment to values, serving the public, an empowered staff, shared leadership, pragmatic incrementalism, and dedication to public service.

The Commonwealth Association for Public Administration and Management, perhaps better known by its acronym CAPAM, studies public management in its 53 member nations. It has written a volume on each of several nations and an overview that points to six essential components of the New Public Management[11]

1   High Quality Services: the association has seen considerable change in the Commonwealth as institutions respond to the higher public expectations with features like the citizens' charters in Britain or the electronic kiosks for license renewal and similar government functions in Ontario – public organizations are setting performance and quality standards, meeting them, and then reaching for higher standards.
2   Dealing with Increasing Managerial Autonomy by Reducing Central Agency Control: special agencies are being created, notably in Britain and New Zealand, with CEOs who can set policy divorced from the central agency, even for personnel.

Some public service commissions are delegating authority to line departments.

3   The Organization and Individual Are Being Measured and Rewarded for Meeting Performance Standards: incentives are considered essential, although Art Stevenson, executive director of the association, notes that "the jury is still out on how effective this has been. At the senior level in New Zealand they would argue it has been successful. On the other hand, the standards are so demanding it is hard for some of the smaller agencies to carry them out." Innovations and award programs have been flourishing, he finds, but not many pay-for-performance programs have succeeded.

4   Technological Resources: technology offers significant potential to make government more efficient.

5   Alternate Service Delivery and Privatization: governments are increasingly asking if they should be in certain activities or whether the service can be better delivered by non-government organizations or corporations.

6   The Purple Zone: the new public managers are concerned about forging a new relationship between politicians and administrators. On this model, the politicians are red, the administrators blue, and the area where they connect is the Purple Zone.

While the CAPAM books discuss public management, they also deal with the overlapping areas of the role of government and the machinery of government.

A THREE-STREAM APPROACH

Over the past decade the Canadian Centre for Management Development, the federal government's school for executives, has taken an innovative approach. It has established an ongoing working group of academics, researchers, and practitioners from six countries who meet regularly to discuss public management issues. Their work crosses all three areas of investigation and has been disseminated in two books, *Governance in a Changing Environment*,[12] published in 1993, and *Taking Stock: Assessing Public Sector Reforms*, published in 1998,[13] both edited by Guy Peters and Donald Savoie.

In their 1993 work they note there is remarkably little effective evaluation of whether the techniques for public management reform being championed in the countries discussed actually work, or whether the gains in performance result from other factors. They note there has been remarkably little evaluation of the implementation process in reforms and the execution of the mandates. Christopher Pollitt, one of the contributors, cautions that we should be careful to distinguish whether reports of improvements are claims from the pulpit by those who preach specific reforms or are based on research or testimonials from people actually within agencies. (He sees more of the first.)

Pollitt also cautions against an across-the-board approach in public service management. He would not want an entrepreneur looking after an aging grandparent, nor a cautious bureaucrat behind the wheel of a fire engine responding to an alarm. Pollitt concludes "the problem is not one of how to apply a magic set of management techniques right across the public sector, it is much more a question of seeking, in each separate case, a match of function, form, and culture. A less rousing sermon, no doubt, but perhaps a more useful one."[14]

Five years later, the same group observes that although no grand design for public sector reform has surfaced, "measures had one thing in common – a strong reliance on the business management model." The literature they reviewed still had very little to report on how well the various measures were working, and they still did not know why some reforms were more successful than others, and why some countries were more receptive to changes than others. Some of the important factors identified by the various contributing authors include:

- The only sin is to be dogmatic.
- Excellent interpersonal skills are of central significance.
- The ability and willingness to communicate clearly and well is significant.
- Champions are needed.
- The manner of implementing reform is important: inadequate preparation and follow-up are common problems.
- In the absence of agreed-on measures, success or failure is often a matter of perception.

In reviewing various reforms, which sometimes took contradictory approaches, they observe: "It appears that almost any administrative reform can work, and equally, any reform can fail, given the particular set of circumstances within which it is attempted."[15] This is consistent with a review of New Zealand's highly successful government-wide reforms,[16] which found the effectiveness depended on execution as much as conceptualization, and that there were "offices that have taken up the challenge and have thoroughly revamped their operations to improve performance, as well as offices that appear to be adrift and bereft of purpose."

In the end this literature leaves us with no clear model of what works, no magic potion that can be applied. We are left with a strong sense that application of a private sector model has had mixed results, but that no one approach can be credited or discredited, because most of the evidence is anecdotal rather than research-based.

That absence of a model, and the mixed results of applying current prescriptions, contributed to our choice of looking at individual organizations rather than country-wide reform, and to the process of asking questions rather than prescribing answers.

Our own study is research-based and helps to bring the focus back to where Brodtrick left off. The sample is international. The organizations are well-performing. They pay attention to nine key areas, most of which have been touched on by other researchers. Our model has a tangible shape and feel that practitioners should welcome because they can understand how the Three Pillars apply to their own workplace. Aim, Character, and Execution are clear concepts, made even more specific and functional, as coming chapters will show, by the nine topics: mission, leadership, accountability, people, communication, trust, management tools, teamwork, and change management. And we have inserted a new element – a questioning spirit – that will be beneficial to public management and, indeed, to public management literature as well. We have added to Brodtrick, as we hope others will add to us.

CAPSULES

- In 1988 Canada's auditor-general found well-performing organizations moving beyond bureaucracy and displaying five common features: emphasis on people, participative leadership, innovative work styles, strong client orientation, and a mindset that seeks optimum performance.

- The few books that are written on public management tend to cover three overlapping areas. One deals with the role of the state. A second grapples with the machinery of government, which is a subset of politics. The third, and least-studied area, is the management of public service organizations, which is our focus.

- Osborne and Gaebler found 10 elements that characterize entrepreneurial-spirited public service pioneers: they steer rather than row; empower rather than serve; inject competition into service delivery; transform rule-driven organizations into mission-driven organizations; fund outcomes, not inputs; meet the needs of the customer, not the bureaucracy; earn rather than spend; strive for prevention rather than cure; move from hierarchy to participation and teamwork; and leverage change through the market.

- The Reinventing Government school of advice might work well in the United States but would have less applicability in other parts of the world since its belief that government must pull back can't be universally applied.

- It's questionable whether a significant performance differential exists between private and public, as some reformers claim.

- Osborne and Gaebler's central prescription of steering rather than rowing is undercut by the fact most of the government operations they chronicled are highly adept at rowing.

- Steven Cohen, in *The Effective Public Manager*, noted that organizations should seek to shape the future rather than be shaped by events.

- James McDavid and Brian Marson, in *The Well-Performing Government Organization*, mentioned that such organizations must reduce barriers and constraints, earn employees' commitment, have effective leadership, provide customer service, and gain central agency and political support.

- Robert Denhardt, in *Five Management Approaches in Public Organizations*, stressed that such organizations should demonstrate their commitment to values, serving the public, an empowered staff, shared leadership, pragmatic incrementalism, and dedication to public service.

- The Commonwealth Association for Public Administration and

Management delineated six essential features of the new public management: high quality services, increasing managerial autonomy by reducing central agency control, measuring and rewarding organizations and individuals for meeting performance standards, technological advances, alternate service delivery and privatization, and the development of a new relationship in the Purple Zone.

- The Canadian Centre for Management Development's ongoing working group of academics, researchers, and practitioners from six countries noted in their 1993 work that there is remarkably little effective evaluation of whether the techniques for public management reform being championed in the countries discussed actually work, or whether the gains in performance were accomplished due to other factors.

- Five years later, the same group observed that although no grand design for public sector reform had surfaced, "measures had one thing in common – a strong reliance on the business management model." The literature they reviewed still had very little to report on how well the various measures were working, and they still did not know why some reforms were more successful than others, and why some countries were more receptive to changes than others.

- Some of the important factors identified by the various contributing authors to those studies include: the only sin is to be dogmatic; excellent interpersonal skills are of central significance; the ability and willingness to communicate clearly and well is significant; champions are needed; the manner of implementing reform is important and inadequate preparation and follow-up are common problems; in the absence of agreed-on measures, success or failure is often a matter of perception.

- Our own work adds three pillars to that literature – aim, character and execution – with nine specific attributes: mission, leadership, accountability, people, communication, trust, management tools, teamwork, and change management. And we have inserted a new element – a questioning spirit.

SECTION 1

Aim

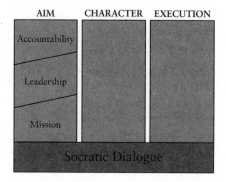

CHAPTER 3

Mission

When Human Resources Development in New Brunswick began strategic planning in the early 1990s, everyone assumed it would produce a flowery and lengthy mission statement that dutifully touched all aspects of the ministry's traditional activities, the distribution of social benefits. But in the middle of discussions, someone suggested a dramatic new vision, summarized in a terse three-word mission statement: "Create Client Self-sufficiency."

New Brunswick had long been an economic backwater, far from the manufacturing heartland of Central Canada, clinging to its base of fishing, farming, and forestry and strongly dependent on the equalization payments through which the country's richer regions subsidize the poorer. But under then-Premier Frank McKenna, the province had been fighting back, gaining self-respect and an improved economy as he courted high tech business. McKenna had recently won his second election, on a platform of provincial self-sufficiency, and expected the welfare machinery to become as modern as the telephone call centres that were setting up shop in his bailiwick.

The proposed mission statement was no-nonsense, like the premier. It fit the electoral platform of the government. And it echoed one of the better known mission statements in the corporate world, Pepsi's "Beat Coke." In fact, it was superior to "Beat Coke" because the steps to achieve client self-sufficiency were less ephemeral and the impact of that achievement would be more valuable to society.

At the Development Bank of the Philippines, the mission statement is anything but terse. It's a 243 word, almost poetic, inspirational message, setting out the benefits to the Filipino people from the bank's new role as a catalyst of the economy. The opening paragraph commits the bank to "a progress achieved by the Filipino's inventiveness, diligence, and productivity ... a progress that ends up in the betterment of the Filipino as an individual and as a people."

The development bank was "reborn" in 1986, to stimulate the economy. If the mission statement is too long to remember word-for-word, its intent is clear and summarized forcefully in the bank's three-word theme: "Country Above Self." Every Monday, employees recite a Family Credo only marginally shorter than the mission statement, much as Wal-Mart employees begin their day with the company cheer. That is followed, in turn, by a weekly commentary on a corporate theme.

Mission statements come in all sizes and shapes. They can appeal to the heart or mind. They can be lofty or prosaic. But in our sample of well-performing organizations, they are ever-present and considered a necessity. All of the organizations but one had a written mission statement – and the exception, Statistics Canada, is headed by a longtime employee, whose speeches and writings on the organization's values have been widely disseminated and serve a similar purpose.

Mission Statement: the Development Bank of the Philippines

The new Development Bank of the Philippines is committed to the Filipino people's progress; a progress achieved by the Filipino's inventiveness, diligence and productivity; a progress providing for the Filipino's basic needs and the higher aspirations of his spirit; a progress that ends up in the betterment of the Filipino as an individual and as a people.

For the new DBP, development entails a willingness and ability to benefit from changes brought about by economic growth translated into: many more meaningful jobs; a wider spread of property ownership among Filipino families; and a fairer pursuit of opportunities through optimum use of one's God-given talents

The new DBP strives to adequately motivate the greater mass of Filipinos to increase their savings to set the pace and influence the pattern of development; to be able to finance long-term investment in productive activities geared primarily towards meeting people's needs.

The new DBP promotes the process of development by deepening and widening linkages: those that bind projects with each other and with their wider environment; those that multiply economic and social returns preferably for the benefit of the poor; into a more interdependent network, whose life and dynamism are thereby enforced.

In facing the challenge of development, the new DBP can only work with others; recognizing the special role others can play, reinforcing the distinctive contribution they can make, being only too conscious of the comparative advantage others have, to be complemented by our own.

The new DBP strives to work closely with entrepreneurs willing to play by the business rules of a market economy; where they aim to succeed mainly through their competitive efficiency; where they relish and exploit the opportunities opened up by changes; where they continue to innovate and prosper.

THE NORTH STAR OF NAVIGATION

Effective organizations must have a sense of direction. And our sample did. They took time to develop a mission and to disseminate it to all employees, whether they were housed in one building or, like New Zealand's foreign affairs and trade ministry, spread out around the globe. When we asked respondents to rank the importance of our twelve areas of focus, they picked mission as the most important.

A clearcut sense of direction is more vital today than ever before because the winds of change are so strong. Nearly three millennia ago, King Solomon, famous for his judgment and good public administration, said: "Where there is no vision, the people will perish" (Proverbs 29:18). The only way for captain and crew to navigate those winds of change is to have, first, a clear idea of where they are headed and, second, a solid idea of the myriad of forces that will influence their journey.

The mission statement is the North Star of organizational navigation (or the Southern Cross, for those below the equator), the luminous reference point by which progress can be measured. It is not a place you will ever reach. It guides you through troubled times. Organizations that fail to pay attention to their overall direction will fall victim to those outside forces. If you don't know where you are going, you are unlikely to get there – and even if you manage to arrive there, you won't know it.

Imagine you're sailing the Atlantic from New York City to Spain, a course that runs parallel to the equator. Assume that throughout the trip the winds are blowing from the North. You don't have to be a sailor to know that if you don't steer northeast for most of the trip, the prevailing winds will deposit you in Africa. In reality, on that trip and in life, the winds swirl around us, blowing from different directions as our agencies voyage along. That makes sensitivity to the winds and the intended direction even more critical. At any point in our journey we can travel in any one of 360 degrees, but only one of those 360 degrees will take us to our destination. That's why modern sailors use a global positioning satellite, adjusting course continuously. They need to know exactly where they are in relation to their intended destination. Well-performing organizations do the same.

A mission statement is the only way to tell the difference between change and progress.

The mission statements of our respondents generally include more than a specific direction. They also display some of the fundamental values on which the organization operates. Our research shows a common set of beliefs must be present within a successful organization. The crew must know not only where they are going but also the acceptable ways of travelling there. This enabling framework of operating values must be taken seriously, by the captain and the crew. Otherwise management's credibility is damaged and the organization becomes detached from reality.

Mission statements can have four different elements, which are often linked:

- the mission itself, defining the ultimate objective;
- core values, which guide the organization in fulfilling the mission;

- principles, which apply each core value to the organization's objectives and programs;
- the strategic objectives, which translate the other three elements – the organizational philosophy – into action-oriented objectives.

The first are three stable, while environmental factors influence the strategic objectives, the basis on which priorities are determined.

SINGING IN HARMONY

Management author Stephen Covey[1] hypothesizes that there is, effectively, a universal mission statement for private sector organizations. We found that, distilled to their essence, many of the mission statements in our sample have a 'universal' theme: they commit the organization and the employees to contributing to society, having a positive impact on the individual citizens they deal with, and continuously improving. Certainly many of the agencies we studied composed similar themes. If the lyrics aren't identical, the well-performing organizations certainly sing in harmony. But each has carefully addressed those universal principles and selected the most meaningful for it, adding some special flourishes that only that group would consider essential to the score.

The internal values of Malta's Management Systems Unit Ltd., for example, are flexibility, commitment, and ownership. The unit strives to be a model of excellence, quality service, professional integrity, and accountability as it delivers technology and consulting services to the public service. It expects employees to be conscious of value for money and cost. The agency's external values indicate respect for diversity of views and beliefs, recognition that everyone can make a difference, and the desire to attain results and accountability through empowerment.

For the 1995-1997 period, the group defined nine strategic objectives. They led off with the intention "to deliver high impact and high-visibility deliverables at lowest cost possible, which will make reform appear more tangible to all and will enhance the image and credibility of Management Systems Unit." As well, the agency stressed the importance of supporting clients in their transition to new technology and of attaining and retaining the highest caliber staff for its own operations.

Some of our respondents have mission statements a century old and, although those missions have been revised, they are still essentially the same as their predecessors. A clear line of heritage remains, rather than an abandonment of purpose, as the agency revises to fit the realities of the day. The Danish Board of Industrial Injuries, established in 1898, was initially responsible for compensation to "injured workers." That was updated in 1933 to reflect the broader notion of injury that was developing and to cover occupational diseases. In 1992 it was modified again, this time to include the modern concern for injury prevention. As well, in this era of heightened fiscal pressures and citizen expectations, the agency stressed that it strove "to be future-oriented and competitive by making correct, quick, and understandable decisions in an efficient and economically justifiable way." And at a time when we're all more acutely aware of the need for exemplary public relations, the board now mentioned the importance of publicizing its role.

The Royal Canadian Mounted Police (RCMP), in its 125th year, points out that missions evolve in step with society: "There is a tendency for social and economic change to take place roughly every 30 years, which approximates one generation. In this century, in Canada, the 30s, 60s, and 90s have all witnessed some degree of social upheaval that has required us to adapt. The ability to adapt but still maintain the same character and purpose is what ensures survival for public institutions."

THE VALUE STATEMENT

Maintaining that character and purpose requires values. Values are the "how" of carrying out the business – the right way of operating. We pass those practices on explicitly or implicitly to new employees because the values help us. Often delineating those values requires brainstorming: in a strategic planning exercise, the organizational values that operate at a subconscious level are drawn to the surface and put on paper for the first time. It's important to ponder what's been omitted and try to fill in the gaps.

The value statement indicates the management team's view of human beings. Are workers considered a bunch of shirkers and sneaks – or is it felt they normally want to contribute and be good performers? How management perceives people – their employees and the citizens they serve – will have a major impact on how those people are treated. What are the most important elements of the relationship with those citizens? What do you think of your employees and how do you wish to relate to them? Those kinds of questions help to define the value base.

In this process, you must also consider how to render accountability to your political masters. Values have to make sense to all the people involved – and they must be prepared to live by those values. What you put in the value statement is a matter of choice, but for a good statement to emerge, some tough discussions will likely precede it.

This process has a bonus: the wheeling-and-dealing power of management is substantially reduced. Without a value statement, managers can essentially do whatever they like, or whatever they think is right, since the organization lacks a clear statement of right and wrong. But if you mark your values down on paper the staff will immediately compare them to organizational reality and a new kind of accountability will close in around senior managers. That is inevitable. It should be expected from the moment the exercise begins. Managers have to make a choice: would they rather be a wheeler-dealer focused on personal gain, or a principle-centered leader focused on making a contribution? They can't be both. Every time they stray from the values, they chip away at their credibility and erode another of the key elements we found in well-performing organizations, trust.

Collins and Porras, in *Built to Last*,[2] stress that core values are an organization's essential and enduring tenets, which are not to be compromised for financial gain or short-term expediency. The authors suggested an organization should have no more than six core values – otherwise they aren't core – and in formulating them, managers should ask: "Which of these values would we strive to maintain for a hundred years *regardless* of change in the external environment – *even* if the environment ceases to reward us for having these values, or perhaps even penalizes us? Conversely, which values would we be willing to change or discard if the environment no longer favored them?"

Values have a tendency to come to life only when they obstruct you. Take the family, for example, that is raising four pre-teens while adhering to the belief that parents shouldn't use corporal punishment on youngsters. When does such a value pop to life? Not when you're sitting around the Christmas tree cheerfully singing carols. At that moment you don't turn to your spouse and say,

"Isn't it nice we decided not to beat the living daylights out of them?" The value springs to mind when one of those youngsters does something outrageous, something you presumed your children could never think of, let alone do. At that moment, when you instinctively feel the only human response is violence in massive doses – that's when the stupid value raises its head and gets in the way. "In our family, we don't beat our children," you remember.

Naturally, you immediately start to argue against the value. It was not drafted with this egregious situation in mind. But that's the point. Values are put in place to stop what you would otherwise feel inclined to do. If you are not prepared to live with the value on bad days – when the kids act outrageously, or the financial pressure on your operation is enormous – don't put it in your personal or organizational mission statement in the good days. Those "times that try men's souls" are, after all, exactly the instances when managers are most vulnerable and when the eyesight of employees is the keenest – and you will pay the consequences if you stray from the promised values. It is better to construct a modest value system and be confident that you can abide by it than to reach for some sparkling principles that you can't meet in pressured situations.

AUDACIOUS GOALS

At the same time, boldness can be a virtue. It can stretch an organization, helping the agency to redefine itself. Collins and Porras found their visionary companies set what they called BHAGS – Big, Hairy, Audacious Goals. Some nations are setting BHAGS and the public service is helping to attain them. In the 1960s, most of South East Asia was slipping, country by country, into civil war, communist invasion, or economic and social collapse. Politicians called it the "domino effect." But in Malaysia and Singapore the row of collapsing dominoes stopped and a profound economic and social transformation was achieved. In the 1980s New Zealand turned around a desperate economic situation and now helps to improve its balance of trade by giving seminars on how to reform and revitalize the public sector. South Africa has, in this decade, set the courageous and dramatic goal of an integrated, peaceful, and prosperous society. The Soviet Union successor nations are attempting a huge leap to escape their past, but are having great difficulty, partly because they lack a well-performing public service and have a less-clear vision of their values and their aim.

One of our sample, the RCMP, started life with a BHAG: to provide police service to the Canadian frontier. An early task was to deal with Chief Sitting Bull who, with hundreds of his followers, had migrated to Canada after the defeat of American General George Armstrong Custer at the Battle of Little Bighorn. The Mounties set another audacious goal: peaceful integration of the tribe into the Canadian West. They determined a strategy – send one lone Mountie. He met the chief and the tribe spent several peaceful years in the country before returning to the United States. Big goals, stretch missions, and creative solutions – public service at its best.

The same process of challenging themselves continues in today's well-performing organizations. For New Brunswick's Human Resources Development, the point of insight that led to its audacious stretch was when it tried to define who its main stakeholder was in strategic planning sessions. Initially, everybody assumed the main stakeholder was the welfare client, the individual in sad shape coming for help. But after much discussion, they realized it was actually the taxpayer. "This was a fundamental, complete shift," notes Deputy Minister Karen Mann. "Times were tough. The mood was mean in the province. We could lose the whole thing."

Initially the mission statement was long and complicated. "Traditionally, everyone has to see themselves in the mission statements in organizations," points out Mann. When the group settled on its clear-cut, single goal, it realized the agency would now have to turn itself inside-out. "Creating client-self-sufficiency is not a typical goal for a social welfare agency. It changes your culture," says Mann.

The Muskogee office of U.S. Veterans Affairs also decided to stretch. When rewriting its mission statement, it chose "to provide the very best service for the military veterans of a grateful nation – the United States of America." By "very best," it meant no less than a prototype government operation. "We didn't just want to be the best in Veterans Affairs," says Vicky Wilcoxen, Total Quality Control co-ordinator. "We wanted to change the way government has been seen to be operating and build a model of how any government work place should be operated. So our model was to think beyond the standard of Veterans Affairs."

Dr Donato Alarcón-Segovia, director-general of Mexico's National Institute of Nutrition, says his hospital "seems to have acquired a soul which is embodied in what is called the Institute's Mystique." The Mystique was written by the founder and long-time head of the hospital, Dr Salvador Zubirán, who attends the all-important graduations of residents, where he personally hands a copy of the Mystique to each of the young doctors. "It has become ingrained in the hospital that there is this Mystique of looking to the best and seeking excellence," notes Alarcón-Segovia.

PROCESS AS IMPORTANT AS PRODUCT

For the RCMP, the process of developing its recent mission statement was as important as the final product. Over 4,300 people took part, more than 20 per cent of the force, through workshops and brain-storming sessions held coast-to-coast by internal facilitators. "Our commissioner turned the process on its ear by having so many people involved," says Assistant Commissioner David Cleveland, the director of personnel. "I would suggest we have a level of buy-in and commitment you would be hard-pressed to find in other organizations."

Initially, a barrage of issues emerged as the staff grappled with the hurt of the past and the frustrations of the present rather than a vision of the future. That's not uncommon: organizations often run into such a barrier in the early stages of the process. When Ole started to develop a mission with the National Parole Board, for example, everyone told him he'd never uncover any values on which everyone agreed. But he traveled coast-to-coast and when he reviewed his notes he found a dozen items on which everyone concurred. For the RCMP, the trick was to get past what became known as the parking lot issues – the complaints that bubbled forth before they could metaphorically even get into the building, let alone begin to plot the mission route. Everyone was patiently heard and, after that initial venting, a list of immediate concerns was shifted to senior administrators for action. Long after the mission statement has been approved, the personnel director and others are still steadily cleaning the parking lot.

Many of the force's mavericks, eager for change, were drawn irresistibly to the mission-development process. They were then invited to serve as facilitators, taking advantage of their energy and encouraging them to view issues more broadly, as facilitators must listen intently to all. Since mavericks often have followings, others joined them in the effort. "While we didn't pursue mavericks, a lot came to the fore," says Commissioner Philip Murray. "They have a lot of cynicism generally but the fact they participated gave the process a lot of credibility."

The resulting statement is thorough, touching all the bases, but not unusual in wording. It includes mission, vision, core values, a commitment to the communities served, and a commitment to the employees. The force intends to be "a progressive, proactive, and innovative organization." Its values will be integrity, honesty, professionalism, compassion, respect, and accountability. Citizens can count on unbiased and respectful treatment of all people, mutual problem solving, cultural sensitivity, and open and honest communications. "If I sat down with my colleagues we could have probably put something similar together in a day and sent it out to everyone," says Murray. "But the process is much more important than the words."

At the same time, he highlights some of those words in the core values. "If we live those values, we will do the right things as it's coming from the inside out. It's not based on some politically correct policy. If you see yourself as trying to make a better society rather than just enforcing laws you will achieve more as a person and as an organization," he says.

Canada's National Library found its value statement treated skeptically at first by employees. Only after time, as management showed it would adhere to those values, were staff willing to take them to heart. In a more prosaic part of strategic planning at the library, figuring out how to divide resources, management decided to unlock their creativity through playing a board game. The National Library had recently held workshops on innovation and creativity so Tom Delsey, director-general of Corporate Policy and Communications, came up with the idea of creating a Monopoly-like game, with cards for opportunity, risk, and various program options. As they played, they talked. As they talked, they better understood each other and the possible organizational directions. They returned to the game in subsequent years as they updated the library's plan. "It helped us to think. It opened up discussion," says Delsey.

In 1992, when New Zealand's Ministry of Foreign Affairs and

Trade was developing its strategic plan, Richard Nottage, the secretary, devised an unusual technique to broaden horizons. He named two separate groups that were intended to compete with each other in producing the best plan. "He was trying to get different ideas. It was quite an interesting approach," says Stephen Jacobi, now deputy high commissioner to Canada but then Nottage's assistant.

IMPLEMENTING THE MISSION STATEMENT

If the mission statement has been developed with a high degree of participation, implementation will already have begun by the time the statement receives final approval. The culture of the organization will have been discussed, increasing staff awareness of direction and method. The organization will feel it is already working towards the desired cultural change and final approval will therefore not be seen as the momentous event that it really is.

With that approval, the plan ceases to be a draft. It is transformed into the most important document in departmental life, apart from legislation. At this stage, the plan requires an enormous amount of management attention since management credibility is on the line. No matter how extensive the participation – even, we suspect, in the RCMP's case – the plan at the outset will still be viewed as management's plan.

As always, effective communication will bring about change more rapidly and more consistently than any other activity. Communication is of paramount importance. You cannot overdo it. The plan must be published and everybody must have a personal copy. Well-performing organizations pursue a variety of other methods for aggressively communicating the plan: speeches, videos, posters, conferences, seminars, and internal newsletters. These all supplement, but do not replace, meaningful face-to-face dialogue.

Properly implemented, the mission will quickly become the department's most powerful management tool. Everything must be re-examined in the light of the mission. Policies and procedures must be systematically reviewed to ensure that they all adhere to and support the mission and strategic objectives. Short-term and medium-term plans must be adjusted to reflect the long-term priorities of the organization. Recruitment, training, and development must be revisited and tucked in line.

The most demanding task, however, is to make the mission part of the overall corporate life. It must become the department's way of thinking, behaving, and relating to issues and opportunities. Well-performing organizations ensure that transformation. The mission becomes embedded in the organization.

No magical method is available for this task. Everyone involved must continually maintain momentum. All initiatives should be proposed and explained in terms of the mission. Issues of concern should be evaluated on the basis of the mission statement. Discussion papers, submissions, and recommendations should not be entertained unless they support the mission. Individuals or groups who take mission-oriented initiatives should be rewarded. And performance appraisals must be linked to the agency's mission.

The importance of mission is stressed in the private sector, but we have repeatedly seen its power in the public sector. In particular, mission statements help staff to fulfill a basic human need to be part of something greater than themselves. Take, for example, the story of the person who passes by three people who are each hammering away at a stone with a chisel. When asked what they are doing, the first person says, "I am chipping away at a stone, as you can see." The second replies, "I am making bricks, as you can see." The third answers: "I'm helping build a cathedral."

A mission statement allows the staff to understand their role in building the cathedral of the well-performing organization. We all want to be part of something greater than ourselves. We want to be proud of our work and the organization that we belong to. We want to be associated with noble goals. We want to build a cathedral. The mission lifts people's eyes from the bottom line to the top line. It doesn't matter whether you are in the public or private sector: You need the magnetism of the fanatic. You must see the cathedral.

COMBATING ROTATION AND THE BIG DADDY COMPLEX

Mission also helps to compensate for the common practice in the public sector of regularly rotating deputy heads. Three or four years might be a long stint as head of a ministry these days. By comparison, Jack Welch, CEO of General Electric, spent his career in GE, and has been at the helm for more than 15 years. The best of the private sector has greater longevity at the top.

Rotation has its advantages. Public service leaders develop a more rounded view of the public service through job transfers. But from the perspective of the individual agency's performance, stability at the top has allure. Missions help in this regard by providing stability. They can replace loyalty to a person – the old guy in the top-floor office – with loyalty to jointly held values and goals.

Missions also boost relations between the minister and the department. Firstly, the staff doesn't wonder who is in charge – the minister or the deputy? Staff focus, instead, on the mission. More importantly, ministers have a right to understand and review the major forces that drive their ministry. But ministers can't have a profound impact on their ministry unless those forces have been clearly identified and described. Most ministers are not chosen to head a department because of their expertise in the issues at hand. Sometimes they have experience, sometimes they are neophytes. Either way, it is disrespectful of democracy for the department not to present clear proposals on where the department should go rather than succumb to the notion that each politician is a "Big Daddy" who seeks only to impose his/her own personal whims on the organization.

The mission serves that function. Politicians respect quality. They detest surprises. If they are offered a non-partisan sense of direction through the mission they will gladly embrace it, obviously adding their own political sense of priorities. That allows the minister to display leadership and set and monitor performance – which is his or her prime responsibility. The minister will also be comforted that, in addition to handling the inevitable crises, the department is attending to the issues that are important without being urgent.

The same phenomenon occurs with central agencies. When they know the department's goals and activities, they are better able to take corrective action. As well, they can support the department in pursuing its objectives (as, in our experience, central agencies generally do). That leads to a more productive and comfortable arrangement. It's also the prime way in which a department can help central agencies to discharge their responsibilities.

That same principle also applies to other working relationships, from fellow government agencies, to private sector partners, to volunteer agencies, to the media and unions. Clarity in direction eliminates unproductive ambiguity and helps everyone to quickly identify issues of concern and opportunities for improvement. The focus shifts from ill-defined problems to well-defined opportunities.

Organizations that know their aim can shorten processes, get to the point more quickly, and produce results faster. It is easier to formulate a project since general directions are known. The feeling that one is always starting from scratch disappears and the necessary level of certainty is more easily attained and maintained.

Finally, environmental scanning is easier and more useful because the organization can identify more accurately what it is seeking. That, in turn, enables it to identify the best possible combination of political priorities, opportunities in the environment, and long-lasting strategic objectives, adding greater certainty to the process. Relevant political signals and opportunities for improvement are detected more rapidly and more unerringly in organizations that are certain about their own direction and confident they are on the right track, like our well-performing sample.

Many poorly performing organizations have mission statements, of course. Sometimes, they're quite fancy ones. But the difference in our experience is that those statements generally aren't treated seriously. With so many more competing priorities in the public sector than the private sector, it's always tempting to deviate from the mission and opt for a short-term salve to a currently vexing problem. But such detours reduce overall performance. We have watched many short-sighted managers assume control of organizations that used to take the mission statement seriously and, rather than supporting this, treat it casually. Performance always plummets.

If the mission statement is currently window dressing in your organization, start changing that. You can begin in your own unit. No unit is too small for such an exercise. You can develop a submission for your unit and rally around it. You can build your cathedral if you start in the same fashion as all our well-performing organizations – by clearly outlining your mission.[3]

CAPSULES

- Mission statements come in all sizes and shapes. But for our sample of well-performing organizations, they are ever-present and considered a necessity – in fact, the most important of the 12 areas we initially focused on.
- It's more vital today to have a clear-cut sense of direction than ever before because the winds of change are so strong.
- The mission statement is the North Star (or Southern Cross) of

organizational navigation, by which progress can be measured. It is not a place you will ever get to. It is something that guides you through troubled times.

- Mission statements vary widely but often contain four linked elements: the mission itself, which defines the ultimate objective of the agency; core values, which guide the organization in fulfilling the mission; principles, which apply each core value to the objectives and programs of the organization; and the strategic objectives, which translate those other three elements – the organizational philosophy – into action-oriented objectives.
- If mission statements are distilled to their essence, a universal mission appears – do good for society, improve the lot of individuals, learn and improve.
- Some missions are still valid after a century of use.
- Maintaining organizational character revolves around values: the "hows" of going about your business – what you consider the proper manner of operating.
- The value statement will indicate management's view of people.
- If you mark your values down on paper the staff will immediately relate them to organizational reality and a new kind of accountability will close in around senior managers.
- Core values are those we would keep for 100 years even if the environment penalized us for having them.
- The process of developing a mission statement can be as important as the final product.
- After implementation, the mission statement requires an enormous amount of management attention since management credibility is on the line. Communication is of paramount importance. The mission must now be made part of the corporate life.
- Mission statements help staff to fulfill a basic need to be part of something greater than themselves – to build a cathedral.
- Mission statements can replace loyalty to a person with loyalty to jointly held values and goals.
- Mission statements help clarify departmental activities for ministers, central agencies, and various external partners.
- Organizations that know their aim can shorten processes, get to the point more quickly, and produce results faster.

EXPLORATIONS

For our survey we asked: *To what extent, and how, does your organization know where it is going in the future? What is its corporate direction or vision...its mission? How does your organization know its identity (for instance, through values or principles ...)? What informs its esprit de corps?*

Other helpful questions might include:

Does your organization have a clear mission?

What process would work best in your organization to create or improve on your mission?

Does your mission speak to your organization's contribution to society, to its impact on individuals, to the importance of getting better at what you do?

Does your mission document deal with the mission, core values, principles, and strategic objectives?

How would you imbed the mission statement in the character and behavior of the organization?

Are you building a cathedral or pushing paper?

CHAPTER 4

Leadership

U.S. President Harry Truman had a plaque on his desk that declared: "The buck stops here." If Dr Donato Alarcón-Segovia had a similar plaque on his desk, it would vow, "The red tape stops here."

Alarcón-Segovia has no patience for bureaucracy. He is a doctor by choice, a leader by default, patiently (and sometimes impatiently) fulfilling his role as director-general of Mexico's National Institute for Nutrition. His love is medicine, not administration, management, or power. "I am the leader but I don't feel much like an administrator. I guide the ship to where it should be in medicine," he says.

His institute's management style might best be called "bush pilot leadership." Its leaders have been an adventurous sort, obsessed with their medical mission, willing to take risk. Alarcón-Segovia remains a throwback to the past when heads of hospitals, universities, and similar public bodies were selected for their medical or academic prowess rather than their management expertise. He leads, yet still carves out sufficient time to see patients and teach. His institute is highly influential, with former staff members now spread about Mexico in positions of medical leadership.

The institute was originally part of the general hospital in Mexico City. But a group of young, U.S.-trained doctors were frustrated by the larger hospital's cumbersome, outdated ways. Fifty years ago, their leader, Dr Salvador Zubirán, who also happened to be personal physician to the president of Mexico, persuaded his powerful patient to turn the pavilion into a separate institute. No money was available for a separate facility, so Zubirán, in his first act of leadership, closed off the connecting link to the hospital by building a fence that forced everyone to approach his new institute by its own entrance. The message was symbolic as well as practical: this was a special place.

Several medical centres opened their doors in those years. This was the last one, the smallest, and the one with the least-adequate facilities. But it was to prove the ugly duckling and become the pride of the nation's institutes, judged number one in the impact of its research by outside evaluators – a special place, in large measure because of its bush-pilot leadership.

Zubirán spent 34 years as leader and has remained an active presence since his retirement. Alarcón-Segovia's voice sparkles when he talks of his illustrious predecessor. Zubirán's Mystique – the mission statement he wrote – and his personal mystique as a leader continue on through the generations, formally recognized by his role at graduation ceremonies for residents.

The second director, interestingly, was a bust. He had risen through the institute's ranks but also served a stint as assistant minister of health. It was felt he became too much of a politician and lost track of the proper direction for the institute. Leaders must stay in synch with the mission and the people. Leaders must also be accountable. With little fuss and through the political strength of Zubirán, he was replaced. The organization was strong enough to survive, and sure enough of its aim to self-correct.

THE MYSTIQUE PERMEATES

Alarcón-Segovia first arrived at the institute as a medical student, rotating through all of the country's hospitals as part of the standard training. "I knew I had come to a better place," he says. "The Mystique had clearly permeated." He was to leave, spending four years at the Mayo Clinic in the United States, but says he was drawn back by Zubirán's bush-pilot appeal to open an immunology lab "for which he had neither the space nor the money. I said I would do it."

The institute has an assistant director who is viewed as its full-time administrator. Alarcón-Segovia continues to research, to attend some clinical meetings, and to see patients three mornings a week. "I learn more about what is wrong with my institute when I meet with patients in the Outpatient Department. Then I come back to my office and call people to fix it," he says. Once a week he tours the institute with the maintenance staff and architects involved in renovations, also searching for what needs fixing.

He views his role and that of his assistant director as carrying the load so others can maintain their medical work. He seeks to make everything easier, not harder. His guiding principle in communications is that not much paperwork must be involved and, if possible, no red tape. Hiring is quick. "If the head of a department requests to hire a person, I say, 'fine. If it's who you need, send me a note and I'll o.k. it.' That's all. I make it as simple as possible," he advises.

But he can't control the national government and its central agencies, with their rules and demands for paperwork. Buying surgical gloves has been a particular headache. Hospitals are supposed to settle for the most economical brand, but the surgeons aren't comfortable with those and it's hard in tendering to specify the subtle difference the surgeons feel. But so far he's managed to win his way for his team.

Pay is poor and to obtain money for extra incentives or equipment the institute has to raise additional revenue from its services. So everyone has been working harder. "It's like the Torrents of Hell. You have to produce more to get beyond the strict budget we receive. And we do it," he says.

The institute is a leader in Mexican health. Others copy its innovations, which pleases him: "We want to trigger change in Mexican health." With its former staff sprinkled throughout the country, the institute has been a school of leadership for Mexican medicine. "If you run a *Who's Who* of doctors around the country, it's our people," he says proudly.

DEFINING LEADERSHIP

Alarcón-Segovia is an unusual leader. But as with all our other well-performing organizations, he's the right person for the mission, the corporate character, and the time. Although leading a hospital is different from leading a police force or a foreign affairs agency or an agriculture department, many of the principles remain the same. Leadership today no longer means simply "getting things done through other people." It is an important factor in shaping an organization, communicating and implementing new strategies, creating new alignments, and building corporate character.

Singapore's Ministry of Defense has thought about leadership, and wants their leaders to:

- involve people and motivate them to invest their personal commitment to the job – that is, to invest the best of their minds and hearts, as well as their hands, in their work;
- be able to provide clear directions and vision for the future of work groups or organizations;
- be masterful at managing interpersonal relationships;
- build good initiators;
- build collaborative, interdependent, and supportive teams;
- manage change and encourage innovation;
- help the staff to find satisfaction in their jobs and promote their personal growth and development.

Leadership helps an organization develop a shared vision and a unity of purpose. It is central to building teams and networks, to forging the all-important trust that binds an organization, and to ensuring the organization has the skills to meet the mission. In an era of relentless change, leadership allows well-performing organizations to maintain their excellence. Leadership is now a strategic instrument, not a personal idiosyncrasy. It is also no longer confined to the top of an organization. Leadership is being found, and encouraged, at all levels.

Obviously we weren't surprised to see leadership emerge as a key attribute of our sample of well-performing organizations. We expected that – as anyone would. But we expected our survey to be replete with references to popular "brand name" leadership styles and to see many of the organizations latching on to one particular style. That didn't happen – and not because this attribute was taken lightly. To the contrary, our respondents put a lot of consideration into leadership. But their eclectic outlook was summed up by Greg Fearn, assistant director of the Program and Policy Analysis Branch of Manitoba Agriculture: "We try to grab the best of management approaches and styles."

We had also anticipated that culture, geography, diversity of service, and domestic politics would result in specific leadership activities or actions that worked in one cultural situation but not another. That happened – but far less frequently than expected.

LEADERSHIP PRINCIPLES

While our respondents weren't devotees of any one theorist, they shared a surprising similarity of leadership approach. Certain principles were repeated by many respondents: listening, involving and delegating, commitment to employees; and consistency.

Listening

Manitoba Agriculture has stressed listening in its leadership style through the influence of a former deputy minister, Greg Lacomy, who headed the ministry from the late-1980s to mid-1990s. "He made it clear to management that the issue of listening was critical. What he had seen with the department and the private sector was that listening is often overlooked in organizations and as a result they are not well-performing," says Fearn.

Listening was talked about at management meetings and quarterly staff meetings. It was part of the skill set sought in new managers. And it continues as a concern, even after Lacomy has moved on. "The current deputy reminds and reminds senior managers to be in touch with middle managers on this. He tells us: Listen to staff," says Steve Washen, a program analyst. Before staff meetings, for example, employees are canvassed to determine what they want on the agenda rather than management presuming to know.

Involving and Delegating

Traditionally, public institutions have been great believers in top-down management. A special Canadian government task force on values and ethics, headed by former Deputy Minister of Justice John Tait,[1] suggested "we would perhaps do well to acknowledge frankly that, because of the structure of political authority and accountability, there will always be a substantive element of top-down leadership in the public service. Being candid about this may be more healthy, in the end, than persisting in a vague twilight in which management practices, including a reasonable dose of top-down direction, are seen by employees as somehow illegitimate or problematic because it is occasionally at odds with more participative and consultative processes."

Our well-performing organizations are not unaware of the need for top-down leadership. But they are more consumed with the value of delegation and involvement. Participative leadership and empowered subordinates are present in each of the organizations, with the goal of having leadership occur at all levels. Peter Underwood, deputy minister of Nova Scotia's Department of Fisheries, told us: "I personally believe that one of the most important attributes in a leader is to be able to delegate. In order to delegate, you must be able to choose good people and be able to tell them where you are going and measure their progress. A successful delegation history is a clear sign of a good leader."

Costa Rica's Civil Service Directorate, which handles a variety of personnel issues for the civil service, is working towards a model of self-management in its own shop: "Each area of activity will be managed by a single public servant, who will then be responsible at this level for implementing the complete administrative process of delivering the required products to the various types of clients."

To attain delegated leadership, Muskogee Veterans Benefits turned its supervisors into coaches. They were told they could only be helpmates. The leadership was to flow from within the teams. The ratio of 1 supervisor for every 9 employees changed to 1 supervisor for every 40 employees – and productivity soared.

The agency also took a leaf from the power structure in universities, where faculty play a self-management role through the academic senate. The Muskogee unit established a Quality Council that acts as a board of directors, forming general policies for the operation. It includes the team leaders, coaches, supervisors, and deputy-director. In fact, all the organization's designated leaders serve on the council except for one person: the agency's director.

The council meets monthly to deal with major issues facing the organization. What would happen if it proposed some action the agency director disagreed with? Would he veto it, like an American president sidetracking Congressional legislation he dislikes? "We don't think we will ever get in a situation where the director will countermand. The things that might not be approved will be worked out through the process," says Vicky Wilcoxen, the Total Quality Control co-ordinator.

Leadership Is Dispersed

That system may seem extreme. Leadership has traditionally started at the top. Most of today's managers grew up with the top-down mindset. The lunatics can't run the asylum, after all. But in our well-performing organizations, leadership is spread throughout the organization. Even the police agencies we surveyed are in accord. The RCMP is obsessed with moving out of a command-and-control mentality, to allow community policing to flourish through self-leadership. The Ontario Provincial Police echoed the Tait Report by noting the need for the "flexibility to move from a command-and-control mode of operation to a participative management mode." It noted that delayering "provides the opportunity and the challenge to empower our people at all levels to make decisions and assume leadership roles."

At the same time, the Business and Technology Integration Group at Ontario's Ministry of Transportation stressed that it's important to balance a desire for involving everyone in leadership with the recognition that some staff are not – and never will be – comfortable in a leadership role. The group recognizes that such people sometimes find it difficult "to find a place in an organization that has placed such a great emphasis on change and leadership."

Rules for Followership

In considering leadership, it's important to remember followership. After all, leaders are also followers. Deputy ministers may sit atop the heap, but when they receive a specific goal from the government for the department, they are both leader and follower. Moreover, as Sam Rayburn, former Speaker of the American House of Representatives, noted: "You cannot be a leader, and ask others to follow you, unless you know how to follow, too."

In *Five Star Leadership*, Patrick Townsend and Joan E. Gebhardt[2] stake out the following ten principles for followership:

- Know thyself and seek self-improvement.
- Be technically and tactically proficient.
- Comply with orders and initiate appropriate actions in the absence of orders.
- Develop a sense of responsibility and take responsibility for your actions.

- Make sound and timely decisions or recommendations.
- Set the example for others.
- Be familiar with your leader and his job, and anticipate his requirements.
- Keep your leader informed.
- Understand the task and ethically accomplish it.
- Be a team member – but not a yes man.

Commitment to Employees

A commitment to employees from top management is also viewed as essential. Public servants are increasingly clear about what they want from their leaders. If received, they respond with performance beyond expectations; if not received, they respond with less-sterling service. The bottom line is that exemplary leadership requires more than cajoling subordinates into mandated activities: it means creating a workplace that is rewarding to employees and helping employees to develop both personally and professionally. It means creating a respectful environment.

Three Types of Consistency

Consistency is an important ingredient of leadership. Leaders in well-performing organizations spoke of three types of consistency:

- the leadership style must be consistent with and focused on achieving the mission;
- each leader's individual style must be consistent with the organization's stated leadership style;
- each leader must be consistent in word and deed.

Well-performing organizations don't tolerate "rogue" leaders. Leaders hold responsibility for ensuring their own actions and the agency's actions are consistent with the mission. They are the main instruments of turning that mission into reality. They begin by taking responsibility for entrenching the mission within the organization and for dealing with violations of it and the core values.

The phrase "leadership by example" popped up repeatedly in

survey responses to describe leadership that mirrors the spirit of the
mission. "It is not enough to talk about values – they must be practiced from director on down," said the U.S. veterans benefits group.
That is a central point today in management literature. Michael
Hammer[3] observes that managers don't just walk the talk but "epit-
omize, teach it, live it." James Champy[4] asserts that "managers can
lead the way – they can model the behavior, enable it, and educate
it, drawing out what is already there, or what they hope is there. In
other words, managers must first change themselves."

Egypt's Cabinet Information and Decision Support Centre was
started by young people in their early thirties who weren't trained
managers, many hailing from academe. Ahmed Nazif, the vice-
chair, had worked on artificial intelligence for his Ph.D. at Montreal's McGill University and was teaching at Cairo University
when asked to help found the centre. Now he's in his early forties
and, like the other top people, isn't much older than his staff.
"Employees see the managers as somebody they would like to follow rather than just as a boss," he says. "We try to make an example of leadership so people can feel they can take a leadership job
soon."

Well-performing organizations also demand consistency across
leaders. Managers are no longer free to select a style at odds with
the values or prevailing leadership style at the agency. These organizations don't tolerate the dysfunction that inevitably results when
followers of Machiavelli, Attila the Hun, Mother Teresa, and
Gandhi all hold leadership positions within the same department.

In the past, a leader was free to operate within his or her own
favored style. If Attila was having trouble, Mother Teresa might
be sent in as a replacement, in a managerial version of the Bad
Cop–Good Cop techniques on television. No more. Well-performing organizations define principles of leadership appropriate to
their particular circumstances, then ensure those principles are consistently applied by all leaders.

Finally, well-performing organizations expect consistency
between words and actions. Their leaders walk the talk – because
they know the walk is what employees watch. "Employees, to
detect what is important, must be able to observe what management does as opposed to what they say," observes Statistics Canada. Failure to be consistent results in a great deal of pessimism and
cynicism about public service renewal.[5]

Taking the Long View

These principles aren't new. They have all been mentioned in the private-sector literature. But it was valuable to document their importance to well-performing public-sector organizations. As well, we uncovered two less-discussed features of leadership that are worth highlighting.

The first was the importance of taking the long view. We were reminded of this again recently when a government scientist was talking about his department's commitment to producing a rust-resistant strain of wheat. Because of the 10 to 15 years required to develop this wheat, no private sector firms were interested, even though the profit payoff could be considerable and the new strain could be used to feed millions of hungry people around the world. But the payoff was simply too far away for the private sector. The public sector, however, isn't driven by quarterly profit figures and on many issues can take the long view.

Psychoanalyst and management scientist Elliott Jacques[6] has highlighted the importance of time – and the long view – in his writings. The man who first discovered the mid-life crisis in the 1950s, Jacques never wrote another word on that subject after his initial groundbreaking article appeared because he was consumed with what he felt was a more important finding in his management studies: organizational hierarchy could be linked directly to time. At each level, individuals must be selected for leadership who have the cognitive ability to deal with the time span of the problems they will encounter. At the bottom of the hierarchy, the longest a decision might impact on the unit is a few days. But at the top, the chief executive takes some decisions that will influence the organization over the next 20 to 30 years and must be capable of grappling with the massive complexity of such challenges. Disasters occur when those at the bottom focus on the future at the expense of the present, and those at the top focus on the day-to-day at the expense of the future.

Many of the organizations in our sample were blessed at birth with far-sighted leaders. Like Salvador Zubirán, they were not "coaches" interested in winning the next game or private-sector clones seeking prestige in the next quarter: they wanted to build an organization that made a long-term contribution to society – to build a cathedral. The top managers in our survey seem to hold a long-term view which expresses itself in many forms, including their preoccupation with principles more than practice when responding to our survey.

The long view also arises in the tenure of chief executives. At a time when rotation is common in the public service, many of our well-performing organizations have had long-term leaders and consider it an important element of their success.

That is consistent, we note, with the research in *Built To Last*.[7] While the business pages celebrate each time a new leader is parachuted in from outside to shake up a company, Collins and Porras found instead that long-serving CEOs who grew up in their organization seem to head the best-performing companies. Rarely did visionary companies reach beyond their own ranks for new leaders and most of the people they picked stayed a long time in office. Again, Jack Welch is a notable example of this twin issue. When GE needed a change agent in the early 1980s, the company didn't go outside: it picked somebody groomed internally, who knew the organization intimately. And he's still around today.

Ivan Fellegi at Statistics Canada is an inspirational example of long tenure in the public service. He has been around as chief statistician for so many years that it's almost impossible to separate the man from the job. He grew up in the organization, starting with it 40 years ago when, as a 22-year-old more interested in poetry than statistics, he joined as a level 1 technical officer. After obtaining his Ph.D. in statistics, he rose through the ranks, to the number two position, almost 25 years ago. He became the ninth chief statistician in 1985. Like Alarcón-Segovia, he is driven by the central mission of his organization – exemplary statistics, in this case. He knows statistics. He knows Statistics Canada. He won't be running a transportation ministry or a trade department next week.

His organization flourishes, even though it's the only one in our sample without a written mission statement, because Fellegi has made the mission and values abundantly clear through speeches, policy, and his own actions. He is a stable element, forceful in expressing his view in simple terms that his staff can understand. He knows everybody in his organization, interacts well with them, and ensures cross-fertilization.

The Statistics Act grants him enormously strong levers to exercise. He is the guardian of core values. He is the final arbiter of statistical priorities. He is the focus of ultimate responsibility for preserving statistical confidentiality. "The Chief Statistician's personal standing is a matter of significance for the statistical system," the organization noted in its survey response. "The Chief Statistician must be ready to place the job on the line as an ultimate protection against the politicization of the statistical system."

That would be more difficult for a chief statistician catapulted in for a two-year term, intended to prep him or her for ultimate glory in Finance or the Treasury Board. It's the long-term leader like Ivan Fellegi, steeped in the tradition of statistics, who protects Statistics Canada and prods it to better performance.

Many police forces today are reaching outside their ranks for new leaders. Politicians appear to consider one police force the same as another for training. But not the RCMP. Its commissioners grew up in the organization – as did the rest of the upper echelon supervising policing. "Everyone who gets to a top position has come up through the ranks. We've done police work. The commissioner has arrested people and been out in communities. This sets us apart from other police organizations," says Assistant Commissioner David Cleveland.

Richard Nottage, secretary of Foreign Affairs and Trade in New Zealand, notes that his ministry has only had five chief executives in 55 years, all homegrown, while many other departments have been headed by ministry hoppers. When the State Services Commission wanted to study long-serving chief executives, it was stymied as only 6 of the 37 department heads had been in office for more than three years.

The problem was exacerbated by New Zealand's 1988 reforms to the civil service system, in which chief executives now sign on for a five-year contract, renewable once for three years. After that period, another search must take place, even if the chief executive has done well and wants to continue; he or she simply becomes another applicant. As well, many chief executives – perhaps recognizing their limited tenure under the system – are choosing to leave for the private sector. "There is a lot of movement," Nottage worries.

Marianne Scott also worries. Canada's national librarian was an outsider when brought in to head the organization a decade ago, but she knew libraries: she had been at McGill University for years in its library system. She recalls it took her six to eight months to know her new organization – even with that extensive background. She acknowledges that management is a skill but insists it's important that leaders be intimately aware of their domain. "I think it is a mistake shifting deputy ministers and assistant deputy ministers around. To me there's nothing like having a deputy minister of fisheries knowing fisheries. He doesn't have to know transportation," she says. "You have to know the organization. You have to know your field. If you've been in a field for awhile your intuition helps you know what's going wrong."

Leadership Beyond Borders

The other distinctive aspect of leadership we detected in our sample was external leadership. These well-performing organizations recognize their responsibilities beyond their own organization. They strive to accomplish more than just delivering the mandated service: they lead outside the organization – in the community and within networks of related agencies. That leadership, interestingly, does not always flow from specific legislated powers but from the desire to more effectively achieve their aim.

Egypt's Information Support Centre is a prime example, shepherding that country into the information age, with the Internet, and consciously seeing itself as a training ground for people who will depart government to work with the private sector. Manitoba Agriculture wants, within its limited resource capacity, to play a leadership role through technology transfer and other means in building a more prosperous agri-food sector. That translates down to the local representatives, who are expected to play a leadership role in rural areas, guiding farmers to more modern and productive methods. "We're encouraging agents of change – people who can facilitate change in their community," says Fearn. We come back to this role, with more examples, in the chapter on communicating and networking.

LEADERSHIP PRACTICES: THE FIVE-STEP APPROACH

Our sample developed their leadership model through a five step process. This approach was clearly defined by the Danish, and it was present, in whole or in part, in most of the organizations:

Step 1   analyse the situation and select a model;
Step 2   provide training in the model;

Step 3   share the model with staff;
Step 4   obtain feedback on application and effectiveness;
Step 5   adjust and update the model.

Long before receiving our survey, these organizations had asked themselves basic questions about leadership. What leadership style matches our mission? What leadership style do our employees need? What leadership style is demanded by the times or the situation? What leadership style do we prefer?

That is in line with Bernard Bass, who in the seminal book on the transformational leader, *Leadership and Performance Beyond Expectations*,[8] noted that leaders must be aware of what leadership is expected of them. For our organizations, in most cases the top management team undertook the analysing and defining.

The mission is one source of information. Employees are another. In 1988, as part of its analysis, the United States Defense Mapping Agency conducted a survey and found employees considered the agency's leadership to be weak. Management responded by implementing a three-phase training program in leadership for all managers.

It's important that leadership respond to the organization's needs at the time. While we have noted the importance of consistency and long-term leadership to our well-performing organizations, it's vital to recognize that over time the demands of an organization will alter. Research on life cycles in the private sector show corporations pass through different stages and different leadership styles are demanded by those various phases. No equivalent research exists on the public sector and our study didn't specifically address the issue, but the premise seems reasonable. Certainly in addressing the organization's needs while developing an appropriate leadership style, the life cycle should be considered.

Our organizations' second step was to train as many people as they could in the desired style. Generally they employed on-site training, with the person who had been trained then helping to develop others. Some of the organizations, for example, trained the top leadership as a team. They then educated people at the next level and it cascaded through the organization.

Sometimes this training is informal. At U.S. Veterans Benefits in Muskogee, they hold brown bag lunches to consider the ideas of the various management gurus, such as Stephen Covey, Jim Rohn, and

Earl Nightingale. Somebody who has studied the expert acts as facilitator of the lunch-and-learn session. Generally the group opens by watching or listening to a tape of the guru before moving on to discussion. Half of the session is on company time, half is on the individual's personal time.

In Denmark, since 1981 all managers must attend a public management course initiated by the government. It's considered a postgraduate program, building on existing knowledge. Individuals can only attend after they have been a manager for two to five years. The eight modules are each a week long, spread over a year. Leaders eagerly await their turn.

Leadership training in these well-performing organizations often involves feedback to the individual, so managers become more aware of their own leadership style and how others receive it. Attila the Hun learns how he is perceived, as does Mother Teresa – and both are expected to adjust if necessary. Research in the 1970s and 1980s found that leaders often rated themselves quite differently – need we say, more flatteringly? – than their subordinates rated them. Employees saw an autocrat while managers saw themselves as benevolent coaches. With feedback on style, through personality tests and employee questionnaires, leaders now get to know themselves better. Then they can work at improving their fit with the organization.

Organizational concern with character and consistency appears to be one reason these well-performing organizations spurn off-the-shelf training selected by individuals and taken individually, off site. Many of those courses are excellent. But while the individual benefits, he or she may be unable to translate the experience back into the organization because the rest of the team is not familiar with the strategy or its key concepts – indeed, some others may have been off at the same time learning a different conceptual model. Taking the same training overcomes that because the program is shared by all and becomes rooted in their behavior.

As well as training managers in a leadership style, the well-performing organizations ensure that all employees are familiar with what they are entitled to. It's not kept secret but shared openly, like the mission. Indeed, everything works in tandem. The mission and leadership style must be linked and the staff must understand the link and see it in operation, daily. In Singapore, for example, the Ministry of Defense holds a two-day workshop for working-level staff on the corporate concept of leadership. The Egyptian Cabinet Information and Decision Support Centre declares: "Any successful organization should ensure that the concept of 'leadership' is very well-defined, understood and accepted among its employees."

The fourth step in the leadership model is feedback. Once the style was set, the leaders trained, and the organization aware of the intention, execution was verified through 360 degree appraisals, meetings, and surveys. At the Central Provident Fund Board, Corporate Planning Officer Celine Tan notes that staff "assess the quality of leadership in their respective department. This helps the supervisor gauge where his/her strengths and weaknesses lie." If necessary, training and coaching follows.

Finally, the agencies adjust. Leadership training is an evolving process and our well-performing sample recognize that. None of them adhere to outdated leadership models. Although "Great Men" founded many of the agencies, leadership is now much more shared. The theories of the 1970s and 1980s have faded. They study the market and keep pace, without being faddish, avoiding seduction by new techniques that don't fit their practical needs.

Leadership Principles
- Listening
- Involving and Delegating
- Leadership Is Dispersed
- Commitment to Employees
- Consistency with the Mission
- Consistency Between Leaders
- Consistency Between Word and Deed
- Take the Long View
- Leadership Beyond Borders

Leadership Practices
- Analyse the Situation, Determine and Model
- Train the Management Team in the Common Model
- Share the Leadership Model with Staff
  - Obtain Feedback on the Model's Use and Effectiveness
- Adjust and Update

All this can help us to improve leadership in our own organization. But most importantly, we must return to Socrates' advice:

"Know thyself." Leadership is not just a process of studying the characteristics of leaders and emulating them. It is not just a matter of learning the techniques of a particular theory and applying them. It is not just a matter of benchmarking the best practices. All of those are useful. But first, it seems, the leaders in our sample have looked inside – inside themselves, inside their organization's missions and values, and inside their organization's workforce and its needs. That has allowed them to find out who they are.

They also recognized this is a life-long process. None of our organizations achieved their current status with a quick fix in leadership – somebody floating in from outside to straighten the organization out. They all found success within themselves. They then went on to follow another sage piece of advice from Socrates: "The greatest way to live with honor in the world is to be what we pretend to be."

CAPSULES

- If Dr Donato Alarcón-Segovia of Mexico's National Institute for Nutrition had a plaque on his desk, it would pledge, "The red tape stops here."
- The Institute's second director didn't work out because he wasn't in synch with the mission and the people.
- Leadership today no longer means simply "getting things done through other people." It is an important factor in shaping an organization, communicating and implementing new strategies, creating new alignments, and building corporate character.
- Instead of latching onto a popular "brand name" leadership style, our organizations sift and blend to develop a management approach that best fits their situation.
- Well-performing organizations ensure their leaders listen. The leaders involve others, delegate, and are committed to employees.
- The organizations prize consistency in three ways: leadership must be consistent with the mission, leaders in an organization must be consistent, and the words and action of leaders must be consistent.
- Many of the well-performing organizations take the long view. Their leadership grew up in the organization. Their chief executives stick around for a long time.
- Our sample recognize their leadership responsibilities beyond their own organization.

- We delineated a five-step model for determining the leadership approach: analyse the situation and select a model, provide training in the model, share the model with staff, obtain feedback on application and effectiveness, and, finally, adjust and update the model.
- Remember Socrates: "Know thyself."

EXPLORATIONS

In our survey we asked: *What kind of meaning does your organization give to the concept of 'leadership;' and how does it ensure that the concept is well-understood and consistently put into practice at several levels of the organization, not just among the top leaders?*

Other questions you might want to consider include:

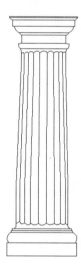

Has your organization thought carefully about leadership?

How would you describe the leadership style in your organization?

Is that style consistent with the mission?

Is leadership consistent across the organization?

Have you received feedback on your leadership, its consistency, and its effectiveness?

Do you understand how your leadership contributes to achieving the mission and how you could better contribute?

Is there consistency between word and deed in leadership?

Does the organization take the long view in leadership?

Would the five-step approach to devising a management style be helpful in your organization?

CHAPTER 5

Accountability

Foreign affairs is generally considered an elite part of the public service. Its interests span the globe. It deals in lofty, somewhat ephemeral issues that require extreme delicacy and flexibility. Secrecy is important, and ambassadors are accountable in ways perhaps less tangible than other departments. Foreign affairs is often seen as "above it all," subject to different rules of engagement. So it may come as a surprise that the well-performing organization that particularly caught our eye for its solid accountability structure was New Zealand's Ministry of Foreign Affairs and Trade. They take the soft, subtle stuff of foreign affairs and fit it into a clear-cut accountability that runs directly from the mission of the government in power down to each staff member.

The value that public servants are accountable is timeless. Benjamin Disraeli, a man skilled at diplomacy and governing, said that power is a trust and those handed that trust are accountable for its exercise: "From the people, and for the people, all springs, and all must exist." His statement is as true today as a century ago when he was British prime minister. But the techniques used to achieve accountability are not timeless. They are rapidly evolving – and for the better.

In New Zealand the transformation began with the 1988 State Sector Act which made departmental chief executives fully accountable for managing their organizations. The chief executive has a performance contract with the State Services Commission, which used to employ and manage the public service as a whole but now simply employs the departmental chief executive and advises the government on public sector management. The chief executive also develops a detailed purchase agreement with his or her own minister, stating what outputs and outcomes are expected in a given year from the ministry. That agreement sets out strategic results that are consistent with the government's strategic direction. And it's not something either can conveniently forget: both the minister and the chief executive sign on the dotted line.

The chief executive then runs the ministry – hires the staff, sets pay rates, and operates free of much of the central agency interference present in other countries. Those central ministries – and the minister – can't keep changing the rules. And it's clear to the staff who is responsible for managing the ministry: the chief executive, not the minister, although the minister remains notable as a prime client. At the same time, auditors from Treasury, the State Services Commission, the Prime Minister's Office, and the Audit Department still keep watch.

"The new system has given chief executives a much greater responsibility to manage resources. The counterpoint is that there is a heavy suite of contracts related to accountability," says Richard Nottage, the secretary of Foreign Affairs and Trade. And the process doesn't stop with Nottage. He delegates down – responsibility and accountability, hand in hand, to fulfill the government's goals.

NEW ZEALAND'S CONVERSION

The process traces back to 1984, when the newly elected Labour government opted for a massive conversion of New Zealand's fortress economy to confront its frightening debt problem. The government deregulated the economy, reduced entitlements, and liberated the private sector. The foreign ministry was originally aloof from much of the tumult. But after awhile the leading reformers – a coalition of young, intellectual cabinet ministers and some talented civil servants – decided that proper economic reform required recasting the public sector, which had grown very large both on its operational and policy sides.

Nottage, a career diplomat, was recalled from his post as ambassador to Japan when he was brought back as deputy secretary in 1988 as the State Sector Act took hold. At about the same time the ministry took over the trade policy functions of the old Department of Trade and Industry. "There always was accountability," Nottage says of the old days, "but there were so many centrally imposed structures. The Treasury and State Services Commission would

decide across the entire civil service the pay raise or the technology
or communications system you could have. One knows where the
buck stops today. One is very conscious that there are big responsibilities to get things right."

He has a long-term performance contract with the commission.
He also has an annual purchase agreement with the minister. It is
kept readily at hand and he is evaluated on it quarterly. The two
negotiate the terms, determining what outcomes are realistic to
expect and how to measure them.

The guiding principle is that if the minister doesn't specify a certain outcome, he or she can't expect it – or suddenly demand it
(although everybody recognizes that in the world of government,
with its emerging demands and political fishbowl aspect, sensitivity is required on all sides). "A minister isn't going to stand up in
Parliament and say we would like to do something about the dying
trees in the national park but unfortunately it wasn't in the contract. But the responsibility for coming up with the money to do
something for dying trees is clearly the minister's responsibility,"
says Stephen Jacobi, Nottage's assistant before becoming deputy
high commissioner to Canada.

The minister of Foreign Affairs and the chief executive continually wrestle with how to develop verifiable performance measures
for their domain. In negotiating a world trade agreement, for example, New Zealand is but one of 187 signatory nations and can't
expect to twist the world around to its needs. The ministry also
can't contract to change the human rights situation in another
country. But influence can be exercised in both situations. Leadership can extend beyond borders. And New Zealand, despite its
small size and geographic isolation, is remarkably present on the
world scene. "It requires care in the way one sets the things we can
do and can't do," Jacobi says. "That has led to quite a bit of real-
ism in the formulation of foreign policy. I heard at a conference I
attended recently that a realist foreign policy is a dreadful thing,
that you can be too mercenary about setting foreign policy aims. It's
great to me. It's exactly what we should be realistic about."

The government might decide to improve its strategic positioning
in the Asia-Pacific region to benefit from expanding economic
growth there. The minister, heeding general government policy,
would then call on the chief executive to expand political and economic linkages with that area. The contract might specify improv-

ing relations with Asia-Pacific countries, particularly Japan and China, and this would then form a specific output in the purchase agreement.

The North Asia Division would assume the challenge, with specific goals for increasing trade and, perhaps, a commitment to arrange a visit for New Zealand's prime minister to that region, including a meeting with Japan's prime minister and key business leaders. The ambassador to Japan now has his goal: to ensure a successful visit and a boost to trade. The deputy chief of mission is then charged with setting the stage for the meetings with business leaders and the various officers who report to him will include their specific, related activities in their own annual performance plan.

In this manner the accountability is translated from a government-wide goal to an objective for foreign affairs employees in the 50 offices around the world. It's backed by an accrual accounting system that tells the government the true cost of managing a particular bilateral relationship. At six-month intervals senior management formally evaluate each unit against the plan, and the performance of individual officers is reviewed against their own plan annually, with an interim report at six months.

THE ROLE OF COMMON SENSE

The system has encountered challenges. In one public department, the chief executive hired as a top operative a person who had drawn considerable controversy over excessive spending while working in another ministry previously headed by his current minister. The State Services Commission, which chooses the chief executive, had to negotiate a delicate compromise. The chief executive had the authority to hire the person, even against the minister's wishes, so it was not reversed, but the chief executive was accountable for the employee's performance. To us, as outsiders, this incident brought out a hard-to-measure but very important accountability: accountability to common sense. Common sense would suggest that a chief executive would only take such action if convinced this was the best person to do the job, and would not do it simply to flex his or her muscles.

Accountability was harder to piece together after a tragedy in which 17 young people were killed when a platform overlooking a waterfall in Cave Creek conservation area collapsed because it was inadequately constructed. Who was responsible for the catastrophe? Who would be accountable? The minister of Conservation, who should have ensured the department was funded adequately? But it wasn't his responsibility to ensure the nails were banged in correctly. Was it the chief executive's responsibility? He employs everybody and should put a management system in place to prevent big mistakes. But he clearly didn't bang in the nails either.

Initially, the top officials, in effect, responded: "I'm not responsible. Blame it on the employee who built the platform." But in the end, everybody was gone, from the person who didn't build the platform properly, through his boss, to the chief executive and the minister, although the chief executive stayed on for awhile to try to rebuild the department. Despite the initial failure of the accountability system to provide accountability, common sense prevailed and many, rather than none, were held accountable. In some cases, accountability transcends the formal contract.

Nottage also goes beyond the contract for his ministry, setting up his own audit team to keep one step ahead of the guardians at the gate. His auditors scrutinize overseas travel, the system for hiring consultants, and other areas of potential abuse. "My team is as astute and acute as anything that can be imposed on me by outsiders. I find that a hell of a comfort," he says, adding: "If there's too much accountability, you can have high compliance costs. That has led us to a new area of risk management. What is an acceptable degree of risk? We don't want a risk-averse culture. We want a nice balance."

DEFINING ACCOUNTABILITIES

Accountability is a timeless value that has often been misunderstood and honored in its absence. It is a sensitive subject because accountability carries negative overtones of control and punishment and is fraught with complicated, and potentially distorting, issues of measurement.

Robert Behn of Duke University[1] recalls serving on a task force which interviewed all the senior managers in a large government agency, with one of his colleagues asking each official: "How does your agency head evaluate your performance?" "It was a most embarrassing question," Behn reported. "Some avoided eye contact with the task force. Some shuffled their feet. None had a clear explanation of how they were evaluated, of how their performance was measured. The best that some of them could offer was: 'Well, I guess if I keep my name out of the newspaper, I'm doing a good job.'"

Behn would get answers from our group of well-performing organizations. Clear answers. Detailed answers. All of our agencies recognize the importance of accountability and have systems in place to ensure staff accomplish more than just keeping their names out of the newspaper. Some are happy with their systems, others are still working hard to improve the process. But accountability is present – and explainable.

Accountability in the public sector is broader than in the private sector. In the private sector, everyone in the company is accountable to its board. The public sector is also accountable to a board of sorts: the minister, cabinet, and legislature. But the public sector has additional accountability to its employees and to its customers, the citizens who use the service – as well as to its non-customers, the citizens who don't use the service. It is a different kind of accountability, more subtle and indirect.

General Motors, for example, doesn't open its books to people who buy its cars. But transparency is valued – and expected – in public service. For example, someone not in jail is free to express an opinion on how jails should be run. An employed person can scrutinize unemployment insurance procedures and talk to his or her political representative about perceived failings in the system. The private sector equivalent would be a Ford owner telling Chrysler how to run its business. Government agencies are also accountable to their partners – the Revenue Department to the Finance Department on how well it collects the taxes that Finance plans on spending, for example.

So multiple accountabilities arise, although the prime accountability in our well-performing organizations is for meeting overall government goals. And it doesn't take New Zealand–style purchase performance contracts for governments to establish that basic accountability. Manitoba Agriculture prepares various reports to the legislature, notably its highly detailed "Supplement to the Printed Estimates," which spells out the expected results of each program in quantifiable terms. It might forecast improvements to the potato crop or enhancements to cash crops due to pest control efforts. The ministry then has to report on actual outcomes, with the Opposition parties receiving copies of all documents. "We are publicly living in a glass house," says Program Analyst Steve Washen.

In Nova Scotia economic growth is a key imperative. The Department of Fisheries has therefore adopted three outcome measures: value of fish exports; value of aquaculture production, and value of non-traditional species production. "These are our departmental masters. All activities must relate to them. It is very simple and effective, especially in a system where monetary incentives are unavailable. The only other incentive is to appeal to people's sense of pride and accomplishment. This is a forceful motivator if well harnessed," says Deputy-Minister Peter Underwood.

It's common to confuse accountability with some sister concepts, authority and responsibility. Authority involves the legal legitimacy to undertake certain actions. Responsibility is the obligation to take care of a certain area. Once you have responsibility you are expected to make a judgment about what part of your authority you need to apply, and how, to your defined area of responsibility.

Accountability follows. If you have authority and responsibility, you also have an obligation to explain how you discharged your responsibility: You must tell your story. But accountability carries a twin obligation: you have to live with the consequences of your actions.

THE GOOD, THE BAD ....

Those consequences might be good or bad. If you have a positive story to tell, the consequences should be upbeat – praise from your boss, a step closer to promotion, recognition in the employee bulletin, an award, or a pay hike. But we generally ignore that positive aspect of accountability, perhaps because we're still caught up in childhood fears. We instinctively associate accountability with being sent to the principal's office for punishment when we were in school, rather than the praise we received from a teacher for our scholastic improvement or from parents for passing a grade. Or perhaps we're haunted by the memory of public service accountability systems that for too long focused primarily on detecting deviation from regulations rather than achieving the aim. Whatever the source, we seem to be more conscious of the negative possibility of accountability than the positive side. In reality, throughout our lives – in school or at work – we generally have a good story to tell and are rewarded in some fashion.

Indeed, most of the time, public servants perform well. They discharge their responsibilities in a totally acceptable fashion and should be proud to tell their story. Even as potentially worrisome an event as appearing in front of a parliamentary committee should be seen as an opportunity to tell one's story – tabling documents, presenting arguments, stating the mission, and describing how well it is being accomplished, demonstrating just how well the department is doing. Sure, sometimes one gets a little beat up, and that is as it should be. Other times the public servant can savor confirmation of a job well-done.

Accountability is the opportunity to achieve that moment of acknowledgment for one's good efforts, at the individual, group, and department level. But to achieve such affirmation, measurements must exist to prove success. Personal opinion is not sufficient. That's where accountability meshes with mission: a clear mission is a prerequisite for accountability. It's not enough to know what we've accomplished. We have to be able to measure and to explain it so that the story makes sense to people outside the organization – including Disraeli's ultimate judge, the citizen.

Famed Milwaukee Braves pitcher Warren Spahn once told Tip O'Neill, then speaker of the U.S. House of Representatives: "Mr. Speaker, baseball is a game of failure. Even the best batters fail about 65 per cent of the time. The two Hall of Fame pitchers here today [Spahn and Bob Gibson] lost more games than a team plays in a full season. I just hope you fellows in Congress have more success than baseball players have." George Will, the political commentator and baseball fanatic, used that anecdote to grouse about the fact that Washington has no .400 hitters and government is therefore spared "the sort of remorselessly objective measurement of their performance that ballplayers see in box scores (in the newspaper) every day."

Behn notes that people in government don't have to wake up in the morning to find out that everybody in the country is reading that they went 0 for 5 yesterday – or, like a corporate chieftain, that sales in the last quarter dropped 15 per cent and the price of shares has dropped. "Nevertheless, leaders in government should want something like that to happen. They should want all of their agency's personnel to read their box score in the morning paper.

They should want all the citizens to read those box scores in the morning paper," he writes.[2]

Well, maybe not every day. Government's work doesn't fall neatly into nine innings – or three hours of daily playing time. Our accountability framework is more complicated than a baseball player's or a corporate executive's. But an accountability structure is possible – even for foreign affairs. And, as with baseball players, it can help to spur higher performance as leaders raise the bar after each season. The agencies in our sample have found a way to measure performance and provide feedback.

The arguments traditionally leveled against accountability have been that you can't measure public goods and that government is a soft, people-oriented service. But public goods can be defined and measured; as Stephen Jacobi points out, it's helpful for that to happen. And although in government we accomplish work through people, so does everybody else, from a baseball manager to a car salesperson. It's often presumed that a car salesperson merely sells automobiles. Wrong. That car salesperson influences people to buy cars, just as we have to influence people to meet our goals.

Indeed, imagine for a moment a world without goals and accountability. Let's say next year we don't count the goals in soccer games or the runs scored in baseball. Would people flock to the games? Of course not, because it would drain the excitement out of the contests. The thrill derives from accountability. And in the public sector, we should crave that same stimulation.

In our experience, public servants want to achieve, to do well, to make a difference. We find they often set goals that are too lofty, that have to be readjusted to a realistic level, since trying to achieve them might only hurt future health and performance. After setting the goals, we also find public servants want results measured. They know that self-praise is hollow. They want objective indicators, so that manager, employee, and public will know when success has been achieved.

Admittedly, sometimes the measures will be soft. Take the classic case of an employee not interacting well with his peers. The manager might have to sit them all down to talk on a regular basis in order to assess if progress has occurred. The results won't be crystal clear. But some broad indication of progress – or failure to progress – will emerge.

... AND THE UGLY

While we have stressed the positive side of telling our story, it's important to remember that some stories will be negative and managers must not shrink from dealing with that unpleasant side of the accountability framework. It's futile to hand out awards at a ceremony if staff aren't also acutely aware that certain individuals had an unpleasant conversation with their manager. Without the tough side, there can't be a soft side. The most powerful disincentive is a manager's failure to hold people accountable for poor performance. Not only do the poor performers continue their ways, the good performers notice and resent it.

If Chester, say, never delivers anything of substance and nobody talks to him about his failings, performance will tail off throughout the organization. Yes, many people believe that good performance carries its own reward. But we are a social species and over time bad work ignored will take its toll on everyone. The psychologists call it external equity: people always ask, "How am I being treated in comparison to my peers?" As the Philippine General Hospital put it: "Managers often encounter managerial and operating problems, imperfections and inefficiencies which if not remedied will deter the attainment of the desired results."

Accountability for negative performance does not require the boss to yell and scream. In most cases, poor performance does not result from ill will or even incompetence but rather from circumstances people have not been able to manage. So instead of responding with an increase in formal punishment, it's better to recognize Chester's poor results as a symptom and try to remedy it through coaching or training. Accountability illuminates these situations, rather than leaving them buried, formally ignored by supervisors but a lingering sore spot for everyone.

Sometimes the organization's managers will be the source of the poor performance. And that lapse can be disguised, appearing to be good performance. Jack Welch, General Electric's CEO outlined that situation in his February 1992 report to shareholders, distinguishing between leaders who were high and low on two criteria: productivity and values. His words, which echo some of the comments in the last chapter on leadership, ring true for the public sector as well:

"In our view, leaders, whether on the shop floor or at the top of our businesses, can be characterized in at least four ways. The first is one who delivers on commitments – financial or otherwise – and shares the values of our Company. His or her future is an easy call. Onward and upward. The second type of leader is one who does not meet commitments and does not share our values. Not as pleasant a call, but equally easy. The third is one who misses commitments but shares the values. He or she usually gets a second chance, preferably in a different environment.

Then there's the fourth type – the most difficult for many of us to deal with. That leader delivers on commitments, makes all the numbers, but doesn't share the values we must have. This is the individual who typically forces performance out of people rather than inspires it: the autocrat, the big shot, the tyrant. Too often all of us have looked the other way – tolerated these Type-4 managers because 'they always deliver' – at least in the short term. And perhaps this type was more acceptable in easier times, but in an environment where we must have every good idea from every man and woman in the organization, we cannot afford management styles that suppress and intimidate. Whether we can convince and help these managers to change – recognizing how difficult that can be – or part company with them if they cannot will be the ultimate test of our commitment to the transformation of this company and will determine the future of the mutual trust and respect we are building. ... We know that without leaders who walk the talk, all of our plans, promises, and dreams for the future are just that – talk.

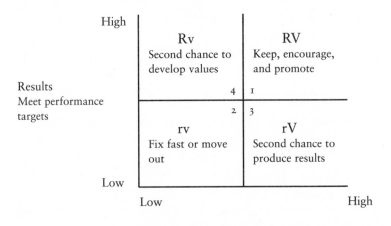

Values
Fit between the individual's values and behaviour
and the organization's values

The tendency in poorly performing public service agencies is to reward the Type-4, who are often, in army terms, good at "kissing up and kicking down," and to ignore those in the second or third quadrant. In the well-performing public service agencies, management is aware of which quadrant each subordinate falls in, and works to move them towards Type-1, as illustrated in the diagram.

INCENTIVES FOR GOOD PERFORMANCE

The organization's accountability system must be set up to measure performance and outcomes, not just to catch deviations from procedure. Too often in the past the reverse has been true. Joy was taken in identifying and blaming those responsible for errors. No equivalent joy was sought in reporting on success. Over time, and in this research, we have seen little evidence that the process of repeatedly embarrassing people by highlighting their flaws will lead to a superior organization.

Conversely, in our sample of well-performing organizations we found a plethora of reward mechanism for good performance, including a surprising number of monetary incentive programs. Traditional public service downplays rewards and seeks to treat employees uniformly. It's feared that the public will be enraged if "bonuses" are paid to individuals for doing their duty. But that timidity flies in the face of the realities of motivation: incentives improve performance. Creative, well-performing agencies seek to establish mechanisms that catch people doing things right and reward them for it.

Private industry coveted Egypt's Cabinet Information and Decision Support Centre staff and lured them with wages that were triple the public service's. The centre responded by boosting salaries and adding incentives that can lift pay to about 70 per cent of the private-sector level. The unusual twist, for a public service, is that half of an individual's possible remuneration comes from the set salary while the other half must be earned through incentive pay. "If you're not really working one month you only get half your salary," says Vice-Chair Ahmed Nazif. Ironically, that means a greater proportion of his staff's pay comes from incentives than is the case in the country's computer industry.

The centre has instituted a fairly elaborate system of performance evaluation that is carried out monthly, eating up about a day of a manager's time. "It kills us in overhead but we do it," says Nazif. When planning, tasks and outcomes are rated on a numerical scale with each month's goal set at 100. If the four tasks for a department in one month were each considered to be worth 25 points and the unit only finished three, the unit would have 75 per cent success rate. Everyone in the unit shares in the distribution of the money, according to the unit's performance.

Denmark's National Board of Industrial Injuries, like other semi-autonomous boards in that country, was given a performance contract that sets out productivity and quality measures. The board handles about 45,000 new cases annually in which a ruling must be issued on the insurance payout by private companies to the injured party. Some cases involve more than one decision, so about 100,000 decisions are taken a year with more than 500,000 letters sent out in that process.

Those figures form the foundation for the productivity measures. But the board is also expected to carry out that work in timely fashion. The average case must be cleared in three months. The most difficult cases must be cleared in nine months.

Outside experts from other government departments also audit 500 cases to check the quality of the information gathered, the quality of the decision, and whether the language used would be understandable by the injured worker. Surveys every second year rate the satisfaction of claimants, citizens, and insurance companies, with the service. Finally, the quality of the board's work is assessed by how many of its decisions are successfully appealed.

The accountability system is new and has prodded the department to improve its case-handling system. New technology has been introduced, work re-arranged, and training increased to boost performance. The satisfaction of a better-performing public-sector workplace is complemented by the same reward as the private sector: profit. The board is given an annual budget to achieve its goals. If it can pull in extra revenue by handling more cases, or reduce costs by automating or not replacing employees who leave, it can retain the surplus, which is then distributed to employees.

New Brunswick's Human Resources Development Department has recently been assigned performance targets for shifting people out of welfare to full-time training and to full-time employment. It was tough to pick a goal for the first year because the ministry has no control over the economy, which can wreak havoc on its plans.

But it met the target of 3,000 people exiting social assistance for full-time work and surpassed its goal of channeling 1,500 people into training – a significant contribution in a province of only 800,000.

The ministry is now introducing a pay-for-performance plan, struggling to apply it to teams. The maximum payout is 4.8 per cent of salary, which can be granted either as an annual increment to salary or a one-time bonus. The department's program is part of a government-wide effort which, interestingly, has drawn no negative reaction from the public. And the process is anything but hidden: all salaries are published and the deputy-minister appears before the legislature's public accounts committee, where she recently took some questions on individual salaries.

Karen Mann also touts the value of old-fashioned incentives. If a team merits a reward, she'll advise them to have lunch on the deputy. "It sounds ridiculous. But that's a real big thing around here. It's a form of recognition. It feels good to send the bill to the deputy minister. It's not lobster or filet mignon – something simple to recognize themselves," she says.

U.S. Vice-President Al Gore showed the value of a cheap incentive when he started handing out Hammer Awards to spotlight individuals and teams leading the way in his efforts to reinvent American government. The $6 hammer is wrapped in ribbon and mounted on an aluminum frame. It symbolizes the dramatic change from the days when the Pentagon managed to pay several hundred dollars each for some hammers.

Muskogee Veterans Affairs has an elaborate incentive system in place that ranges from monetary awards to balloons. Traditionally the unit had a basic reward program tied to the annual performance review. But as it revamped operations and adopted a team-based approach, incentives had to be reformulated. Teams set short-term goals based on organizational objectives; if met, they receive money, certificates of achievement, or time off. Some awards come from the director's office, but others might be on-the-spot from the managers. The team itself is handed some cash to distribute to individuals it wishes to recognize, either from its own ranks or from outside, when somebody from another team offers it valuable assistance. Those awards can't be willy-nilly: the team must establish criteria and the person being honored must have met the goals of providing value to the organization and improved service to customers.

If something notable happens, cakes are bought to reward a team. When the education team was ranked the best nationwide in veterans benefits, management ordered a cake big enough for its 180 members to celebrate. In lesser instances, balloons might be placed in the work area of a praiseworthy team. "They and their peers know they are being recognized," says Vicky Wilcoxen, the Total Quality Control co-ordinator.

Finally, when teams report to the director by e-mail, he speedily sends out congratulatory messages by the same route. "We try to focus on giving positive feedback in as many ways as we can," says Wilcoxen. "They appreciate these efforts almost as much as the money. To have an effective recognition program doesn't take a lot of moolah."

She's had to heed her own advice lately. Previously the agency had eliminated a bundle of supervisors and liberated that money for overtime and incentive awards. "We paid out more incentive awards than any other VA office and at the same time had the lowest cost per employee of any VA office in the States," she notes. More recently, however, the parent organization has been micromanaging the budget and monetary rewards will be rare. But the balloons and congratulatory messages will continue.

Revenue Canada redesigned its award program with a three-tier approach that allowed for local recognition, regional recognition, and an annual national celebration of the best of the best. The program will include peer recognition and upward recognition of supervisors by their staff. The ministry is also contemplating a survey to check the program's effectiveness by asking staff if they feel they are being recognized when they should be.

In developing the program, Revenue Canada realized that the various awards wouldn't be sufficient without an everyday effort at recognition by supervisors. "Recognition to be effective has to be a practised competence of the management team. It has nothing to do with the trinkets you give away or taking people to dinner," says Bruce Veinot, acting assistant director of the ministry's Service Quality Development Unit.

ACCOUNTABILITY MUST BE FOCUSED

We were impressed by the focus of our agencies on accountability. They tied their accountability structure to the mission and the values. They narrowed down their critical performance indicators, not saddling themselves with a million things to measure. They also accepted that some things may not be measurable but can still be important. If they agree at the management table that something is good, then it is good. After all, we know the difference between a good and a bad bottle of wine, even though we don't all have a chemical analyzer at home to generate precise tannin readings. Accountability must reflect that reality: sometimes the people who are experts in a field – those leading an agency – are actually in the best position to judge quality performance by an agency.

We were impressed that the agencies didn't flood us with auditor-oriented responses. The best accountability systems recognize, as Henry Mintzberg noted in the *Harvard Business Review*,[3] that "control is normative ... rooted in values and beliefs." Otherwise, gameplaying will occur as people try to rearrange their outputs and activities to maximize personal reward, rather than achieving the agency's aim.

That was vividly illustrated by an auditor who was reviewing the perimeter security of one of our penitentiaries. He could find no flaws, so he asked the officer at the gate to allow him into the vehicle inspection area. The officer obliged, but in the process violated the rule that staff must enter through another door. Naturally, that one induced-error was central to the report.

The story didn't end there, however. Subsequently, in tit-for-tat retaliation, the officer insisted on searching the auditor's vehicle, which was parked on the penitentiary lot. In the trunk, in the auditor's suitcase, was a bottle of whiskey. That broke the regulation that alcohol must not be brought onto prison property. So the auditor was reported and the whiskey confiscated. This is a merry tale, oft retold, but the point is that none of it contributed to beneficial accountability.

OVERCOMING HINDRANCES TO GOOD MANAGEMENT

When well-performing organizations encounter an impediment to good service, they don't whine or complain, nor do they simply accept it or ignore it. They manage with integrity and awareness of the company mission, seeking ways to change the impediment, knowing the accountability systems will honor their mission-compatible actions.

At Manitoba Agriculture a local foreman wanted a winter coat to be placed in a truck used by several staff members. Unfortunately, his department's regulations didn't give him the authority to purchase a single coat, although it did grant him the right to establish a clothing issue for all employees in his group. In other words, he could buy twelve coats but not just one, since that was presumed to be inequitable. The resourceful foreman resolved the matter by ordering a "protective warming device" for the seat of the truck, which he was entitled to do. The device just happened to be a winter coat. In this case, the foreman's desire to do a good job overcame the inertia of an outdated, control-oriented system and he was celebrated by his managers in their response to our survey. In a less-robust culture one would expect the control system to triumph and the service to suffer.

It should be a duty for every public servant to identify and eliminate such hindrances to good management. Sandford Borins, a professor of management at the University of Toronto and Edward Warrington lecturer in public policy at the University of Malta, in summarizing the 1994 conference of the Commonwealth Association for Public Administration and Management, concluded that "if managers are to achieve exacting service standards, they need increased autonomy, particularly from central agency controls, so they can use their expertise and creativity." We started this chapter with a prime example: New Zealand. But most in our sample have managed that, to some extent. Some are newer, smaller agencies set up outside the usual bureaucracy. Others are older, established agencies that have set themselves off from the rest, and yet others are finding ways of coping within larger, traditional bureaucracies. Clearly the trend is toward mission-focused accountability and away from central agency interference and traditional accountability approaches.

Departments must follow the government's strategic aims, and ministers have a moral duty to put in place the policies they were elected on. Without a mission, it can be damaging when leaders are obsessed with the shifting political winds or a minister's personal agenda. One of our respondents, at a meeting of agency heads, was struck by how they live and breathe according to what the minister needs politically. "I was quite saddened. I remember the kind of public service dreamed of in the 30s and 40s, where they could give advice to the minister, speak truth to power. Now they aren't. They try to take the temperature of the minister before they speak. I was appalled by it."

That does no good for anyone. But with a mission, and an aim, the minister and the department are better able to incorporate and achieve legitimate policy changes, enabling them to be responsive to and respective of the political authority. The mission helps the minister put competing forces in perspective, bearing in mind the overall agenda. It also creates a point of departure for new ideas. A change to the mission statement is quickly communicated and given high profile, in contrast to more traditional and less effective ways of trying to change destinations, or change course.

It's important that managers recognize all their accountabilities. Sometimes it's to mission, sometimes to the minister, sometimes to outside bodies and sometimes to subordinates. Managers need to define expectations in all those cases so they can manage effectively. Accountability runs up and down the organization – and to the outside. Together with mission and mission-focused leadership, accountability rounds out the picture, and defines the aim, as our well-performing organizations aptly illustrate.

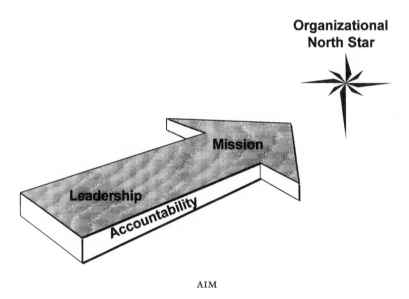

AIM

CAPSULES

- The value of accountability is timeless but the techniques are rapidly changing – for the better.

- The key to New Zealand's accountability system is a purchase agreement in which the minister and chief executive sign on the dotted line. The outcomes are then translated down to individual employees. It's backed in foreign affairs by an accrual accounting system that tells the government the true cost of managing a particular bilateral relationship.
- Accountability is a sensitive subject because it carries negative overtones of control and punishment and is fraught with complicated, and potentially distorting, issues of measurement.
- The public sector has multiple accountabilities – to the government, citizens, outside agencies, and employees – although the prime accountability in our well-performing organizations is clearly to the overall government goals.
- If you have authority and responsibility, you also have an obligation to explain how you discharged your responsibility. You must tell your story. But accountability has a twin obligation: you have to live with the consequences of your actions.
- Public goods can be defined and measured, as our agencies show.
- Managers must not shrink from dealing with that unpleasant side of the accountability framework.
- In our sample of well-performing organizations we found a plethora of reward mechanism for good performance, including a surprising number of monetary incentive programs.
- Recognition, to be effective, has to be a practised competence of the management team.
- The best accountability systems recognize that control is normative, rooted in values and beliefs.
- When an employee knows enough to turn a winter coat into a protective warming device, the accountability system should reward rather than punish him.

EXPLORATIONS

In our survey we asked: *How do you ensure that your organization is able to focus on issues (operational issues as well as policy issues), values and principles, and results? How do your accountability, incentive, and reward systems reflect the importance of attending to issues, values, and results?*

Other questions that might be useful include:

Has your organization properly defined account-abilities?

Are systems in place to monitor achievement of the mission and provide feedback?

Are the right things being measured?

Is recognition practised?

Are incentives in place for good performance?

Is bad performance dealt with?

Do you know where each of your subordinates is on the Results-Values chart? What can you do to move each into the preferred quadrant where they deliver on commitments and live the values?

SECTION 2

Character

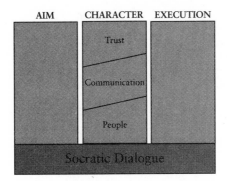

CHAPTER 6

People

In the world today, nobody has job security. Like everyone else, the people at Statistics Canada are starkly aware of that: they've seen colleagues in other departments laid off and their own agency has studied the corporate and government downsizing phenomenon of the 90s. Contrary to the trend, Statistics Canada formally adopted a no-layoff policy in 1978 and has maintained it for permanent staff throughout the lean-and-mean 90s while other departments were shedding people. The staff at Statistics Canada understand they don't have absolute job security. But they come as close as possible. They know the chief statistician, Ivan Fellegi, and his management team, are doing everything they can to preserve jobs and provide a people-centred workplace.

"We're very, very different," says Eve Simpson, chief of Human Resources Strategies. "Dr Fellegi believes you have a career at Statistics Canada. We pick the best people. You come in and we have methods to move you around the organization. He really seems to believe it's far better to have people grow and be flexible than to bring people in for a short time and then throw them away. We're not disposable. We're meant to be kept. It creates security."

We've all heard the phrase too many times: "People are our most important resource." It spills off the tongue automatically these days. In many organizations those words resemble reality only in the most tentative way. But at Statistics Canada, and our other well-performing organizations, management takes the words seriously and goes to great lengths to let the people know they are the most important resource.

Statistics Canada, remember, is an agency with clarity of vision despite not having a written mission. Their response to the survey captures their vision of people and stakes out the range of personnel issues all well-performing organizations face:

The Agency views Human Resources Management with specific goals: getting the best people; training them to do their jobs; organizing them to make the best use of their talents and to ensure co-operation; promoting career-broadening experiences to make the best use of their potential so to prepare our future leaders; and creating a supportive environment which will encourage best efforts and retention.

The Agency's basic philosophy is one of placing a high priority on these human resources functions, not only because they guide us towards an equitable and civilized way of treating people, but because this is the best way to obtain maximum performance and to strive for and achieve excellence.

Statistics Canada has attained excellence through the work of its people. It has been twice named the top statistical agency in the world by the hard-nosed *Economist* magazine.[1] But what's also notable about the people-oriented policy is that it bonds staff to the agency as a whole, rather than their own particular corner, or profession. That's even more significant because Statistics Canada recruits specialists – notably economists, statisticians, social scientists, and computer experts – who might be expected to focus narrowly on their niche. But the people at Statistics Canada are taught to think about the whole agency, through programs that also try to meet their personal needs for stimulation and self-actualization.

It starts at the start, with recruitment. And yes: the agency has managed to recruit, despite its no layoff policy and a string of tough budgets, by preparing in advance and managing attrition well. As its work force ages, the agency strongly believes its future effectiveness depends on attracting the best new professionals available. "Even when funds were very, very tight, we continued to recruit, even though we knew it would be costly. We knew in the long run we needed it," says Simpson.

In the old days, individual managers hired for their own slice of the agency. Now, managers indicate needs but the recruiting is agency-wide. And the people hired aren't immediately slotted into a department. They begin their work at Statistics Canada by rotating for the first two years through a variety of departments, to understand the full nature of the agency. After all, they are intended to last.

The new hires are generally at the top of their class and hold graduate degrees. Economists, for example, have a master's degree with an A- average or better. They are also chosen for flexibility, because that will be demanded of them in this agency.

During the initial two years they are assigned mentors, who will indicate when it's time to shift to another area. They also take two types of formal training: individualized for their current assignment and common flagship courses in such generic matters as survey skills and data analysis. Those flagship courses are so popular that when they were initiated for newcomers the existing staff insisted on – and received – similar offerings to advance their own knowledge. "Things evolve and grow in Statistics Canada," says Simpson.

The training and flexibility is all the more important given an analysis the agency conducted of its vulnerabilities. The study revealed that the age structure in senior ranks might precipitate large-scale retirement within a relatively short period. The threatened loss of human capital intensified the need to make the remaining people more versatile and to increase performance. The agency reacted: the average number of training days for permanent staff more than doubled.

A management committee supervises training, led not by a human resources functionary but by a line manager. It is felt that line managers understand the needs of operating departments better and can proselytize more effectively for new initiatives. They also keep the red tape to a minimum.

That philosophy has helped in the agency's CAD program, which brokers loans of employees to new jobs in other areas of the agency under the aegis of the Corporate Assignments Division, which gives the program its name. The idea here is to invite and encourage employees to broaden their horizons and spice up their careers by taking assignments in new arenas. The program also meshes perfectly with the imperatives of a project-driven workplace. The assignments are arranged through a consultation process between the home manager, the host manager, and the assignee – but when the negotiations need a nudge, it helps that the program's head is a line manager with a commitment to rotation.

When the program began, some managers blocked the process,

trying to hang on to employees. "So Dr Fellegi came up with the four-year rule. If you've been in your job for four years you have the right to go. It doesn't matter what your supervisor feels," says Simpson.

The employees who try the program are guaranteed total job security – after all, this is Statistics Canada. If the assignment doesn't pan out, they can return to their old job, which is still considered theirs. At any one time, 500 permanent employees – or about 10 per cent of the work force – are on assignments of anywhere from six months to two years. The message, says Simpson, is clear: "Go out and try something different! If it doesn't work, your old position is still there. Give it a try. Why not?"

Those principles apply in management selection and training. The agency has adopted generic competitions for promotional opportunities at levels like director, assistant director, and section chief, in which staff members don't apply for a slot in a specific division but for the general managerial position. That offers greater formality and transparency, largely overcoming the problem of "crown princes and princesses" being given a leg up by their enamored boss. It also opens up more chances for those seeking a promotion, as they can apply each year for the generic competition and might be slotted into a job outside their normal division.

Divisional directors and deputies are rotated through the agency, again to enhance career development. Rotations take place at variable frequencies, but for assistant directors three-year assignments are the norm. The relation between assignments is intended to be a logical one rather than being dictated by the happenstance of vacancies. People first.

So amidst the overall employment security, a lot of job shuffling actually takes place. The two, after all, must go hand in hand, as the agency adjusts to the changing environment by retraining and reassigning. "We know we have to be flexible. We joke about the Rubber Band Man – from the song," says Simpson, referring to a jazz standard of the 1930s, popularized again by Rickie Lee Jones in the early 1990s. "But we're willing to be flexible. We know we're career public servants. But that doesn't mean the same job for life."

The organization also honors staff, with a special event near Christmas in which various awards are handed out, including for meritorious work by groups and an Employee of the Year. The celebration takes a full morning, presided over by the chief statistician.

"There is a ceremony to it," says Simpson. "It has a homey feeling even though there are tons of people there."

In 1992, in the midst of the North American recession, the agency surveyed staff, asking if they were satisfied working at Statistics Canada, with 73 per cent replying affirmatively. In 1995, 85 per cent said yes. The improvement resulted from these programs and from a people-oriented approach that was highlighted by the job-security stance of the chief statistician. "We all wondered: would the policy have to go? Seeing Dr Fellegi do so much to keep the policy standing has been a cornerstone for esprit de corps and trust," says Simpson.

Fellegi and the organization he leads have *character*. That's not a word that generally shows up in the management literature. And we stumbled upon it unexpectedly. Reading the voluminous replies took, literally, weeks. Re-reading, trying to understand, we began to visualize the individuals who led these organizations, people we were meeting in most cases for the first time, through their writing. From their words – which described their actions and concerns – the image emerged of leaders of enormous strength of character, grounded in fundamental values such as integrity, being trustworthy, and paying attention to people. Clearly this was a pillar of good performance.

Amidst our era's massive change, the traditional basics of good individual character – honesty, integrity, and reliability – remain rock steady. Similarly, the basics of organizational good character remain consistent: caring for employees, a zest for communications, trust, honesty, openness, and a quest to improve. Given the underlying universality of human truths, it is no surprise that well-performing organizations around the world pay attention to similar aspects of their character.

The Lebanese Civil Service Board, like public service commissions around the world, has the mission of recruiting, selecting, training, and protecting the rights of public servants, in order to provide the best possible employees for other agencies to meet their mandates. During a quarter century of war, through their buildings being bombed, their staff subject to sniper fire, they continued, steadfastly, in the direction of providing, developing, and protecting employees of the public service. Their remarkable story is one of courage, of literally strength under fire. That's something we expect of our armed forces, but not of these civil servants. Even though, on a world class scale, the Lebanese Civil Service Board might not be in the first rank, we can learn from their courage and commitment – their strength of character.

A lot is heard these days about culture, which is easily confused with character but is actually quite different. Culture is weaker and glitzier. Culture can be as simple as men wearing long-sleeve dress shirts with a tie, and a jacket which is hung up on arrival at work and not put on unless you are attending a formal meeting. Character is who you are. It's a much stronger, deeper concept. Stephen Covey, at an individual level, makes a similar distinction between personality-centred leadership and principle-centred leadership.[2] The latter you can almost feel, and touch. The former glitters, then fades.

Many cowboy entrepreneurs in the private sector, of course, have character – and often are characters. So character can take on different flavors. But for our exemplars of public service, character boils down to wanting to improve society through their work and through the manner by which they accomplish their work. That can best be achieved in a workplace that is enjoyable to be in – where colleagues are constantly improving, and open and honest with each other.

That character is generally readily apparent to outsiders. We have spent a lot of time in correctional institutions. Our service at one time had a huge manual with over 500 standards to guide assessment of whether a jail was good or not. Interestingly, however, a perfect correlation existed between the institution's ability to comply with those standards and a few simple factors that hit us within five to ten minutes of entering the prison.

At the entry point, where visitors are searched, one can immediately sense whether the staff are professional, competent, and friendly. Do they thoroughly complete the full search, as they should, even though one is a visiting dignitary? What interaction was there with inmates? Were their eyes down and did they avoid looking at staff and visitors – or if they looked, was it a glare, a snarl? – a solid indicator we'd find a lot of non-compliance with the regulations. But if the inmates were friendly, initiating eye contact and perhaps saying hello, and if the staff were similarly friendly and courteous, generally at the end of the actual audit we would find the institution performing well. In effect, those first few minutes revealed the institutional character, and the performance was invariably related to the character.

Organizations without character are like dysfunctional families, with a lot of dishonesty and personal agendas. They're unpleasant places to work. They are unpleasant places to visit – the specific sites that when encountered by the public inspire the general disdain that so many citizens harbor towards the public service.

We have highlighted character at an interesting time, since a renaissance around values and principles is currently springing forth. We see it on the bookshelves with the phenomenal success of books like *The Celestine Prophecy*,[3] the *Chicken Soup for the Soul* series,[4] *Reclaiming Higher Ground*,[5] and Stephen Covey's principle-centred writings.[6] People are seeking meaning. They want to lead value-centred lives. And that includes work. The age of Aquarius is already being felt.

An essential ingredient of our well-performing organization's character was the attention paid to people. Indeed, of the 12 management issues we initially focused on, these organizations rank the "people factor" as the second most important consideration, after mission. They also recognize that room for improvement will always exist in dealing with people. It's a domain in which management can never do enough – that no organization can ever get just right.

"Work is not only to make a living, it is also to make a life," stressed the Development Bank of the Philippines, the agency with the poetic mission statement reaching to higher values. "DBP, therefore, exercises not paternalism but tough-minded respect for individuals to grow in self-reliance and responsibility. ... The reality to most adults is that they work at least eight hours a day, five days a week in the same place, which demands that the workplace be an achieving environment. The DBP philosophy in the workplace is therefore consistent with the natural family's role of inducing the full development of the person."

The value for people came out in remarkably consistent ways for our sample. Listening. Developing people. Delegating responsibility and trusting staff to perform competently. Providing meaningful work: "It is gratifying to work in the public service, because we work for the good of society, not just personal gain," wrote the Swiss Federal Environment, Forests, and Landscape Board. In organizations that talk about people but don't follow through, a different flavor exists.

Some critics suggest that it's easy for the public sector to be people-oriented, because it doesn't have to turn a profit. The public sector can therefore move more slowly, take more time to nurture staff, and spend more money at it. That claim is doubly wrong, however. Budgets and time pressures are fierce today in the public sector. People policies don't come easily. Agencies have to work diligently at this issue – as Statistics Canada shows.

But the flip side of that cynical assumption is also erroneous: the implication that well-performing companies in the private sector can't afford to pay attention to staff. Collins and Porras[7] found their top companies focused intensely on people – and were wildly successful economically. Bill Pollard of Servicemaster, in *The Soul of the Firm*,[8] describes how one of the world's most successful companies has its mission etched in stone at the entrance to corporate headquarters:

> To honor God in all we do
> To help people develop
> To pursue excellence
> To grow profitably.

Well-performing organizations in both the private and public sector share this people-oriented approach. It is a key to success, not a byproduct.

In this vein, sound human resource policies are critical. Our well-performing organizations don't treat such policies as an afterthought or an obligation – or as the special province of the human resources department. For example, the head of human resources in New Zealand Foreign Affairs and Trade is always drawn from the ambassadorial staff. "You don't want someone making your HR policy who is not a diplomat," says Stephen Jacobi, the deputy high commissioner to Canada.

The emphasis on people must transcend policy. It is personal, not just corporate, caring. Dr Donato Alarcón-Segovia of Mexico's National Institute of Nutrition has spent a lot of time trying to help a secretary with a hyperactive child find an appropriate school. In the past, his institute hosted an art class for children of staff. If they found a particularly gifted youngster, the institute would offer a scholarship for university studies in art. "I try to look to personal matters," he says.

As with Statistics Canada, our sample of well-performing organizations were very conscious of the need to avoid layoffs, and many managed to avoid them by skillful budget management and planning. They also paid particular attention to recruiting and staff retention. The Business and Technology Integration Group of Ontario's Ministry of Transportation tries to break the mold in recruiting. It seeks individuals who are willing to express and support a forceful opinion – but not dogmatically. Their role is a technological catalyst, handling service delivery for the ministry through automatic-teller-like kiosks and other ventures, yet they prefer recruits with business skills over those with purely technological expertise. "They can, over a short time, learn the technologies. But learning the business approach takes longer," says the group's director, David Mee.

The Norwegian Petroleum Directorate fights to keep from losing staff to the industry it regulates. The directorate pays much higher salaries than the civil service, in order to be competitive. For the first ten years of a specialist's career, the salaries between the directorate and the industry are now equivalent. However, after that point, industry pays better and woos the top performers. The directorate's main defense is the quality of its workplace. It tries to offer staff considerable responsibility, international work, and even a chance to be well-known, as an incentive to stay.

Those defensive maneuvers have been reasonably successful – to the point where even people resigning report that they consider the directorate a superior workplace. We found, overall, that those agencies that were able to compete with private sector salaries kept their staff. Those that could not compete recruited the best, kept and developed them for five to ten years, then replaced them with the best young recruits when they moved on.

At Veterans Benefits in Muskogee, employees are given the freedom to complete their work at any point between 6 a.m. and 6 p.m. In Denmark, the staff of the Industrial Injuries Board can choose the hours they wish to work from 7 a.m. to 7 p.m. while working the core hours of 10 a.m. to 3 p.m. If the employee has children under the age of 3, however, they are not bound by the fixed time slot.

In return for working longer hours to improve service, any staff member of the Injuries Board can also take five Care Days every three months – no questions asked – for any family obligations. Those are available in addition to days off when a child is sick – and the 12 days leave that a parent is granted during the first three years of a child's life. As well, children are welcome in the work-place in emergencies and the board has various toys and computers with games for such situations. "It provides the flexibility for the families to function," says Marianne Hvolris, the head of Information Technology.

The board has a physiotherapist to deal with injuries to its own staff. It also subsidizes massages for employees. "It's part of every-day life. If you have trouble, you call the physiotherapist," she says.

When the RCMP found that some of its aboriginal recruits from the Arctic were unaccustomed to the food at their training courses, it flew in seal and caribou meat to provide a familiar diet. When the officers asked for a boot designed a specific way, the force ordered the boots, then changed the type of boot again when the officers were not happy with the boot they had asked for. Attention to the little things accompanied the agencies' attention to the big picture.

The well-performing agencies had an array of social activities for staff (Figure 6.1). Generally they were coordinated by employee committees, making the ventures sensitive to staff needs. We were initially puzzled why social and athletic events were more popular among agencies from smaller, more tightly knit societies. Larger, more impersonal urban communities had fewer such activities than we expected.

Family-Friendly Workplaces

A variety of culturally sensitive initiatives in our well-performing organizations make the workplace and after-work hours more family-friendly and socially supportive. The goal is to facilitate the ability of employees to raise their children, to provide social activi-ties, and to create a family-like atmosphere at work – to make it possible for employees to combine family and work life in the best possible way for them, adjusting to their individual circumstances. Some examples:

- ballroom dancing lessons provided by the Philippines General Hospital;
- flexible work hours provided by many;
- sports and cultural activities sponsored in Egypt, Malta, and the Philippines;
- healthy lifestyle programs in Singapore;

- family outings – picnics, sports events, cultural events;
- ergonomic work places and equipment;
- fitness centres on-site;
- mental health support, physiotherapists, employee assistance programs, specialists on site or available on contract to deal with the stresses and strains arising from either the workplace or home;
- summer school for the arts, cinema club, art exhibits;
- improved food and music in the staff lunch room and lounge.

Figure 6.1

In the end, we think the reason is that the workplace enhances what employees already value. In societies where after-work social activities are primary, the workplace contributes to that value; in less-personal urban situations, where commuting is a complication and a time-muncher, the workplace focuses more on supporting child-care arrangements and matters that contribute to the employee's chosen lifestyle. They provide on-site day care instead of trying to assemble an agency soccer team.

The sample organizations devoted considerable attention to training, again through a variety of methods. The most awe-inspiring effort had to be the Egyptian Decision Support Centre's agreement with the Mastrich School of Management in the Netherlands to provide a special MBA program for 40 of its young leaders in one burst. The eighteen month course was grueling for all concerned: "We had managers yelling at us as the people in the MBA program were working for their departments only 25 per cent of the time," recalls Vice-Chair Ahmed Nazif. But in the end all but two passed, and the organization had a more capable workforce.

The Defense Mapping Agency in the United States, which supplied timely cartographic products to the U.S. military before merging into a new agency, regularly selected employees to attend full-time educational programs, usually at the graduate level. Typically, 50 employees were attending two-semester courses at any one time. It also actively promoted a tuition-assistance program for those wishing to attend after-hours classes and installed a distance-learning centre for those not able to attend on campus. The agency didn't just focus on its professional work force but also extended upgrading opportunities to clerical employees. Each year clerical staff were given a chance to attend college classes to improve their ability to compete for advancement.

Some of the well-performing organizations offer paid and unpaid sabbaticals for research and professional development. Often the organization covers the employee's tuition costs and the employee is guaranteed a job on returning to the agency – refreshed and replete with new knowledge.

It's hard to mention the word people these days without the word empowerment. That's not a word we favor, however. It feels like something managers do to employees. The notion of empowerment brings to our mind those old pictures from Strasbourg, France, of force-feeding the geese to have their livers grow – stuffing things down their throats, in our best interest, not theirs. People don't need empowerment in that sense. They need room to maneuver, room to grow. The old-fashioned concepts of delegation of authority and trust capture the desired approach.

In culturally diverse areas – particularly English-speaking and European countries – our agencies placed emphasis on having the workforce representative of the public. Traditionally, women, cultural minorities, and aboriginal people have not been represented in the public service in proportion to their numbers in society. So special efforts are being made to recruit and retain them. The motivation was partly rights-based but also partly a recognition of the contribution more representative teams can make.

While our organizations stressed people, and tried to meet their needs, the organizations also recognized, as shown by the rankings, that accomplishing the mission is number one. Peter Underwood, of Nova Scotia Fisheries, stressed that striving to make people the most important resource "does not mean that everyone must be kept happy all the time or that people must always have their way. In fact, the people are the most important resource but they are not the most important aspect of the organization. The people are there to serve the goals and mission of the organization, whatever they are. These must come first – and they do in our organization."

Mission first, followed by people. Of course, inevitably it's all linked. People produce the mission, provide the character, and pursue the strategy. Focusing on people has a bottom-line impact on everything else. The agencies in our sample seem to act in a corporate way on what are their personal values for the growth, development, and well-being of their staff. They do it because it's the right thing. But it is also a very good business decision. In the public service, people truly are the basic asset. Building that asset base is good public service management.

CAPSULES

- At Statistics Canada and our other well-performing organizations, management takes serious the words "people are our most important resource," and goes to great lengths to let the staff know it's true.
- Statistics Canada sums up people-work as follows: "The agency views Human Resources Management with specific goals: getting the best people; training them to do their jobs; organizing them to make the best use of their talents and to ensure co-operation; promoting career-broadening experiences to make the best use of their potential so to prepare our future leaders; and creating a supportive environment which will encourage best efforts and retention. The agency's basic philosophy is one of placing a high priority on these human resources functions, not only because they guide us towards an equitable and civilized way of treating people, but because this is the best way to obtain maximum performance and to strive for and achieve excellence."
- Statistics Canada shows how employment security and job flexibility must go hand-in-hand. Also, it demonstrates how to combine a broad view of the agency with individual development and self-actualization.
- Amidst our era's massive change, the traditional basics of good individual character – honesty, integrity, and reliability – remain rock steady. Similarly, the basics of organizational good character remain the same: caring for employees, a zest for communications, trust, honesty, openness, and a quest to improve.
- Room for improvement will always exist in dealing with people. It's an area in which management can never do enough – that no organization can ever get just right.
- At Development Bank of the Philippines: "Work is not only to make a living, it is also to make a life."
- The valuing of people came out in remarkably consistent ways for our sample. Well-performing organizations listen to people. They develop their people. They delegate responsibility to them and trust them to perform competently.
- Our well-performing organizations didn't treat employee policies

as an afterthought or an obligation – or as the special province of the Human Resources Department.
- From flex hours and Family Days to ballroom dancing and massages, our agencies have a slew of people-friendly activities.
- Well-performing organizations devote considerable attention to training.
- The agencies delegate to staff and give them room to maneuver.
- For our sample, mission comes first, followed by people – who make that mission come to life.

EXPLORATIONS

In our survey we asked: *The phrase, "Our people are our most important resource" is one of the most frequently found 'slogans' in the world of organizations. However, in many organizations those words only resemble reality in a very tentative way. Some organizations seem to like the words better than the reality they are meant to describe; other organizations take such words very seriously and go to great lengths to ensure that their employees, at all times and under all circumstances (also in times of contraction), feel that they are the most important resource. How would you describe your organization in this area?*

Other questions that might help you better understand the 'people' in your organization include:

Do you feel valued at work?

What contributes to that feeling?

What can be done to improve the way people are valued in your organization?

CHAPTER 7

Communication

One of the secrets to the Norwegian Petroleum Directorate's success is location. When the agency was established to regulate the oil industry, head office was placed in Stavanger, on the coast near the North Sea oil fields, rather than in the capital of Oslo, where every other public service department was headquartered. The result has been better communications with the oil industry and better customer service.

Oslo and Stavanger are only an hour apart by plane. In 1972, when the agency was founded, that wasn't a great distance and in today's era of e-mail and teleconferencing it has grown even shorter. But the psychic distance is considerable. "If we were in Oslo, we would be influenced by the central government culture and its values. That would create habits of acting. We for sure would have acted in a government way and be dealing more with the politicians than the industry," says Paul Bang, head of the strategic planning section. "The clerks in Oslo do their business to satisfy the politicians. We do our business to satisfy the customers – the industry – as well as the ministry."

The location encourages more informal communications with the industry, as staff from both sides bump into each other in Stavanger and chat. Formal sessions, which often require a large number of people, are easier to schedule, since everybody's in the same city. Meetings occur more frequently. "It's easier to deal with your customer if he's next door," says Bang.

Well-performing organizations are moving away from a fortress-like, come-to-me approach. They are striving for easier physical contact, and therefore better communication, with their public.

Community policing, storefront welfare offices, electronic kiosks in shopping malls, tax offices with convenient, speedy access – the new approach is contagious in the public service.

Internal communication and communication with partners are also important. For Revenue Canada, one of the secrets to internal communication success has been serendipity. From 1992 to 1995, as the 40,000-employee organization restructured, the number of internal newsletters mushroomed. But instead of those newsletters being mandated from on high, most were grassroots, initiated by concerned employees who wanted to connect and communicate. Indeed, the birth rate was so high that management studied the boom to come to grips with it. Eighty newsletters were in existence, close to half born in the previous few years as anxiety over downsizing and reengineering rose. The bulk – 65 out of the 80 – were in regional outposts, away from Ottawa, suggesting that internal newsletters help geographically dispersed offices keep in touch on a personal and professional level.

The personal was as important as the professional, with 81 per cent of newsletters reporting on social information as well as more formal office matters. The newsletters were valued by staff, promoting cohesiveness, stimulating new ideas, and communicating timely information. They were also decidedly local: the content related directly to readers, reporting news about their colleagues and their immediate work environment.

Were they costly? Not really. Volunteers carried out most of the work at home or outside the office, with an editor steering the newsletter as part of work-related duties since the publication was generally a work tool. The *Dominion Bugler*, in the small city of Belleville, Ontario, cost $21 for photocopying 175 copies every quarter; no staff costs were tallied up since everybody volunteered their own time – and even their home computers – to the project. The *Origin Bulletin*, produced quarterly for a 650-person trade administration branch, cost $2,500 in salary and $758 for printing per issue.

"Internal or employee newsletters are considered to be good investments of time and effort. They are flexible tools which allow downward, upward, and horizontal communications," the study decided. It then closed with a list of outcomes that reads like a checklist of internal communications needs for organizations: "More specifically, survey respondents indicated that internal newsletters are recognized as a means to combat rumors, correct misinformation, build support for organizational positions on issues, explain human resources issues, build esprit de corps and pride in work, improve morale, explain technology and how it works, improve customer service, stimulate interest in excellence, encourage the desire to improve and adopt new ways of doing business, relate organizational goals to employee interests, and recognize outstanding performance."

THE MANY FACES OF COMMUNICATIONS

Communications is one of the more-complicated issues facing management because it has so many facets. Internal, external. Planned or crisis response. Newsletters. E-mail. Meetings. Brochures. Posters. Media interviews. The list goes on and on – and on and on.

But the biggest problem is illustrated by the very definition of the word communicate. At one level, communicate means "to make known" and "to transmit to another." At another level, the dictionary talks of an "interchange of thoughts" or "to be joined or connected." It's easy to communicate, if communicating is simply transmitting messages. It's harder to arrange for those communications to produce a genuine interchange – to connect people and ideas and values.

"There is a point where you can communicate downward to your heart's desire and people don't want to listen. At certain points you simply twist yourself into a knot," laments Marianne Scott, Canada's national librarian. Tom Delsey, her head of Corporate Policy and Communications, nods in agreement: "It's a case of repeating, repeating, and repeating."

Well-performing organizations do exactly that. They employ an arsenal of materials and channels – from electronic newsletters to tea with the boss – to network with and serve their stakeholders. Most of those methods are highly familiar to anyone who has ever worked in an organization. But if the channels are many, the process is anything but haphazard. These organizations attack communications with the same vigor and rigor applied to the other nine key elements we've delineated. "You can never over-communicate in a time of change," says Dorthee Bouwhuis, a senior planning and projects officer with Revenue Canada. "If you have no news, tell them you have no news."

The survey showed there is no best way to communicate. Organizations that don't have a newsletter are not necessarily poor communicators and organizations in which a random selection of employees drink tea with the manager are not necessarily paternalistic or old-fashioned. In all well-performing organizations, however, managers spend time thinking about their communications needs, identify methods, and execute.

In our survey, we asked about external relations separately. But organizations saw external relations as part and parcel of their need to communicate, so responses about that issue are included in this chapter, as are some thoughts on "customer satisfaction."

THE BUBBLE CHART

The first step in communications is to figure out the audience. For that, we recommend a simple technique called the Bubble Chart, which is used in sociology and architecture to map relationships. We have used the Correctional Service of Canada bubble chart (Figure 7.1) as an example. The Commissioner, the chief executive, connects with his management team, staff, other deputy ministers, central agencies, the police, the public, and the media, to single out just some of the main players.

Organizations have bubble charts and so do individuals. All the relationships on your bubble chart must be managed. Whether it's another agency, a subordinate, a superior, or the citizen standing at a wicket expecting service, you must manage the communications and, indeed, the entire relationship, so that the stakeholder is satisfied.

For that, we recommend a useful formula:

$$S = P - Ex$$

in which S is satisfaction, P is performance, and Ex is expectations. The level of satisfaction, therefore, is determined by performance minus expectations. Or, more succinctly: to satisfy someone we must ensure that the performance exceeds expectations. Much of this book focuses on increasing performance – and hence, satisfaction. But it's also important to realize, as our formula demonstrates, that expectations are critical to stakeholder satisfaction. Too often, we overlook that crucial element of the equation. We don't take

CUSTOMERS EXTERNAL TO GOVERNMENT

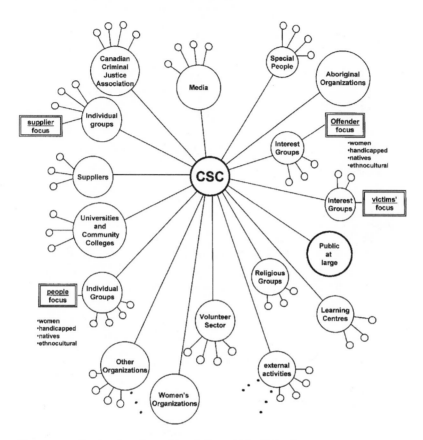

Figure 7.1 Correctional service of Canada bubble chart

time to discern the expectations of everyone on our bubble chart, let alone try, when possible, to reshape those expectations so that they are more achievable.

Some managers are meticulous about their connections. They know all the stakeholders, and how often to communicate with them. Certain ones might be seen for lunch once a year. Others might participate in a daily or weekly meeting. But a systematic plan exists for everyone. And in encounters there is a steady give-and-take to understand and manage expectations so that consensus exists on the desired level of performance and what is achievable.

CUSTOMERS EXTERNAL TO CSC, INTERNAL TO GOVERNMENT

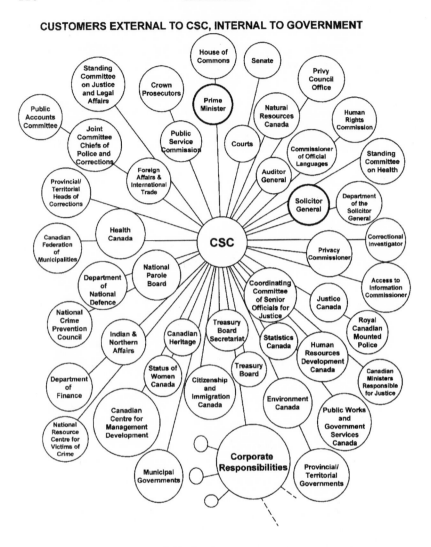

In some ways, that may be the most basic communication for a manager – understanding expectations, communicating what is possible, and reaching agreement on satisfactory performance.

Sometimes the question has to be asked quite bluntly: "Just what do you expect of us?" Correctional Service, for example, has a government-appointed critic, the correctional investigator, who checks out complaints from inmates. His annual report doesn't always delight correctional management, in part because it catalogues their shortcomings. But even here, it is important to define expectations.

"What would it take," Ole asked once, "for you to write next year that our department has made the greatest improvement you have ever seen?" That's the level of performance managers should seek. But it needs to be defined, beforehand, with a clear exchange of expectations.

One of the great mistakes managers make is to assume other people are mind readers. They take it for granted that just because the manager wants some outcome the staff will know exactly what to deliver, even though it hasn't been defined. At the heart of managerial communications, therefore, should be an effort to develop precision around goals, accountabilities, expectations, and the day-to-day operational hurdles.

For that, face to face communication is ideal. Ontario Transportation's David Mee picks the time that colleagues will be most available for such personal contact. Generally, he finds the beginning or end of the day is best. That's when he'll roam, meeting with people he needs to reach. "It's something I have grown up doing and try to continue. It can create a sense of interest and trust and commitment."

"It's important," he stresses, "to remain positive in such sessions. In a government setting these days, the atmosphere can often be unsettled. It's easy for personal contact to slip into unconstructive complaint sessions, leaving everyone unhappy." Mee compares such situations to the age-old question of whether a glass is half-full or half-empty. "You have to take the opportunity to fill the glass half full," he warns, "to communicate success as well as to understand failure."

MANAGING AN AGENCY'S STANDING

Statistics Canada takes great pains in managing its standing and reputation. That begins with the relationship to central management agencies. But it extends to other government agencies, the public, and key users of statistical reports. Every time a statistical release is issued with some significant and non-routine information, for example, the chief statistician sends a personal letter containing analytic highlights to the deputy ministers of appropriate government departments. To support planning, the release dates for the most sensitive data, such as unemployment figures and consumer prices, are announced each November for the coming year.

Since most people obtain their statistical information – and form their impression about Statistics Canada – through the media, the agency pays particular attention to the Fourth Estate. The organization's daily publication summarizing new statistical information was refocused away from the purely descriptive – what went up; what went down – to become more journalistic, with a story line that emphasized insights and significant new findings. That wasn't left to chance, either. For one year, the chief statistician and some of the agency's best analysts spent several hours each week critically reviewing the latest releases. Needless to say, that provided both guidance and motivation for staff to adopt the new orientation.

Statistics Canada operates a highly regarded hotline for journalists seeking statistical information, swiftly linking them to the designated experts. Senior economic columnists attend background briefings on the merits and limitations of major statistical products. "The importance of perceiving the statistical office as a well-managed agency cannot be exaggerated," Eve Simpson, chief of Human Resources Strategy, writes.

The National Library is systematic, perhaps because it's also in the information business. A number of years ago it adopted a set of guidelines for internal communications that was distributed to all staff and is given to newcomers at their orientation session. The operating premise is that communications within the library should be open and pro-active, with everyone – managers and staff alike – sharing responsibility for communications.

"The guidelines make it clear that staff are expected to make their information needs known to those they work with and that they are expected to cooperate with supervisors and managers in setting up mechanisms to facilitate internal communications. The onus is then on staff to use those mechanisms to obtain the information they need; to share the information with those who need it for their work; and to cooperate in resolving communications problems. Staff are also expected to report relevant information obtained outside the organization," the library states.

Management responsibilities are also spelled out in the guidelines. Managers meet with staff to identify job-related needs for information and to establish appropriate mechanisms. They also ensure that staff know how to use the information mechanisms in place, and that supervisors and staff fulfill their individual responsibilities for communicating with one another.

The library has a checklist for managers to review information needs with staff. It prepares an annual communications plan. And it is super-careful about any written material that communicates policy, to ensure accuracy. "Once you put words to paper you can't take it back. There is a process that is followed and heaven help the manager who screws up," Scott says.

Scott also recognizes her relationship with other libraries in the country, meeting regularly with their CEOs at various association meetings. "Having coffee or dinner, you pick up all sorts of things," she says. "And they sense that the National Library is approachable."

Other agencies went to great efforts to obtain external verification of their success. Some, such as hospitals, sought accreditation under relevant standards. Others sought out private sector validation, such as the ISO 9000 qualification or Ford Foundation, Deming, Baldridge, or Presidential Quality awards. Such independent recognition helps establish and maintain the agency's standing with its partners and customers.

TAILGATE (AND OTHER) MEETINGS

All the well-performing organizations have regular meetings to share information. The Northwest Territories Workers Compensation Board in Canada's Arctic holds daily "tailgate" meetings, named after the practice in the construction industry of the foreman starting the day by sitting on the tailgate of his or her truck to issue the daily assignments and deal with employee concerns. Gerry Meier, board president, started the practice when he joined in 1992, having seen the value of such informal sessions when he worked for Imperial Oil in the mid-80s.

Initially, everyone at the compensation board gathered and he would pass along any new information and give other managers, staff, or groups like the social committee a chance to address the clan. Even though the board has grown significantly in size and 90 people now attend, the sessions are short – 5 to 15 minutes. In fact, it has worked so well that his managers insisted on hosting tailgate sessions with their own departments, so Mondays and Wednesdays are now full board sessions while Tuesdays and Thursdays are departmental sessions. Meier tries to inject humor, if possible. "When people leave the room to go back to work, anything you have done to raise morale is time well spent – particularly in the long winters up here," he says.

Egypt's Cabinet Support Centre, spread out in nine locations across Cairo, brings managers and unit heads together every Wednesday morning for an 8 a.m. breakfast followed by a one-hour meeting. Usually one specific item is discussed, a project or strategic issue on which everyone should be briefed. The presentations are scheduled 20 weeks in advance, although more urgent matters are slipped in as required. At Mexico's National Institute of Nutrition, the staff gathers Friday mornings from 8 a.m. to 9 a.m. to share information, mostly on medical issues. The Philippine General Hospital uses meetings as its principal method of internal communication: "They provide participation, give members a sense of belonging, and are excellent distributors of information."

Manitoba Agriculture makes a point of taking management and staff from its various units on visits to other branches so that they are familiar with each other's work. The policy group might spend a day with the operations group at the local university where the veterinary services and animal industry branches are located. After meeting, the visitors tour the veterinary and dairy labs.

The RCMP, with officers spread through all the nooks and crannies of the world's second largest country, has made extensive use of Town Hall Meetings, in which officials meet with everyone from a detachment and answer questions. Commissioner Philip Murray has averaged 100 town meetings a year – about two a week, somewhere in the far-flung country, where he outlines his strategy and opens himself up to be grilled by his officers on any issue of importance to them. It's a huge commitment of time. But Murray doesn't give it a second thought. "It really pays off," he says.

Muskogee Veterans Benefits holds quarterly employee forums, in which the only representatives from management allowed to attend are the top two: the director and his deputy-director, who runs the day-to-day activities. The director updates staff on current matters and then opens up the forum for employees to air any concerns they wish in the absence of their direct bosses. "It depends on what's in the air. But it's not heated. It's always a discussion," says Vicky Wilcoxen, Total Quality Control co-ordinator.

Of course, not everyone can always attend meetings, particularly in places like hospitals or a police organization, with 24-hour-a-day operations and emergencies to respond to. The Defense Mapping

Agency's major facilities were equipped with an internal cable television system, generally in operation around the clock. It showed live and taped briefings and conferences. That was particularly advantageous for people on the second and third shift. The broadcast system also reminded staff of important upcoming meetings and events.

THE ELECTRONIC REVOLUTION

Our questionnaire arrived in agencies just as use of the Internet and e-mail was taking off. Many were already on board. By now, no doubt virtually all use this new form of communications extensively, which can be both a blessing and a curse. Communications, to be effective, have to be targeted. Too many organizations and individuals are just dumping information.

E-mail can be a prime example, with reports being dispatched willy-nilly and staff sending their opinions to top officials three times a day, intending to show how brilliant they are but actually only triggering extensive use of the delete key. At the outset, organizational maturity can be tested by this new device. But at Muskogee Veterans Benefits, e-mail has been used to open the director's door even more to staff. They are invited to e-mail him about anything, at anytime. They do. And he responds. "It keeps steam from building up," says Wilcoxen.

E-mail and the Internet open more than the director's door: it is possible to reach all stakeholders, easily – assuming they complete the communications transaction by reading the message. This electronic revolution will continue to transform many public servants' jobs. Stephen Jacobi, from his perch serving New Zealand in Canada, points out that "electronic communications run the risk of making diplomats irrelevant. You don't need me to send New Zealand a policy of the Canadian government by fax as it's on the Internet before you blink."

Communication should be focused, and purposeful. It's important in this era of information overload to control your own time – for this activity and others – through strategic agenda-setting. For example, rather than mindlessly responding to other people's requests, establish goals for how to apportion time and review the distribution of recent months. Sometimes the situation has changed and what needs attention needs to be rejigged. Frequently the scrutiny serves as a reminder of activities that are not receiving enough attention.

Most managers would benefit from adopting such a technique rather than just aimlessly moving through their work days. Otherwise the individual assumes he or she is a leader but in reality is little more than an elevated switchboard clerk, not achieving his or her own work ambitions. Communication, which helps us to achieve our work goals, is double edged; it can also be the main impediment to achieving those work goals, if we are not careful.

Measuring communication effectiveness can be difficult. Internal communications is a particular quandary since it's a convenient whipping boy. If staff don't have anything else to complain about, they raise lack of communications. We've all heard the complaint: "They don't tell me anything!" Well, maybe they tell that person a lot but he doesn't read it. Or maybe they tell her too much, so she doesn't have enough time to sift out the important stuff. It's important to determine the actual nature of the problem, keeping in mind that communications-related criticism is not necessarily a bad thing. It can be a sign that staff are short of other things to complain about.

It's impossible to tell everybody in an organization everything. If managers did, staff would spend their whole day reading somebody else's views rather than carrying out their own mission. Communications is a constant struggle about how much, what format, and to how many people. "One group says you're burying us in paper out here. Another group will say you never tell us anything," says the RCMP's personnel chief, David Cleveland. "The middle ground is to develop an effective means of communications with people. We're getting there."

EVALUATING COMMUNICATION EFFECTIVENESS

Some of our well-performing organizations evaluate their internal communications by staff surveys. Informal monitoring can also be effective. It is useful, when talking with employees, to ask about key messages management has been sending out. Have they been received, understood, and accepted? If the boss has been delivering speeches on risk management and that theme has also been underlined in the weekly bulletin or other communications vehicles, do staff have some sense that the topic is important?

A large or diverse agency like foreign affairs or a national police force has to ensure management's message is consistent geographically. We heard recently from a manager who attended a speech given by his boss on a key corporate issue what was intended as a complaint but we took as a compliment: "It's the same speech he gave to the people in the western region." Exactly. The organization's leader has to say the same things in each bailiwick. The organization must be consistent.

In reaching out externally to customers-citizens, public service organizations have been abandoning the 1960s model for communications outlined in J.D. Thompson's classic work, *Organizations In Action*.[1] It was based on the principle that good public servants wanted the least interference possible from external sources. They would operate like the assembly-line workers of Henry Ford and Frederick Taylor. Each public servant would be an expert in his or

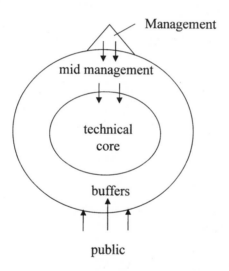

Figure 7.2 Traditional public service organizations

her small field and would concentrate on that territory for their career. Together, those experts formed the technical core shown in Figure 7.2.

Those experts would be surrounded by – and protected by – a group of middle managers, flacks, and palm-wavers, known as the buffer. They would insulate the experts from the changes taking place in society, so the staff need not respond on a daily or hourly basis. The theory was that if you had been hired and trained to be an expert in your field – be it a correctional officer or statistician or passport clerk – you could now keep on doing your job, unchanged until retirement. After all, you were an expert.

The model actually worked well, for the times. It increased efficiency. It helped some people who were not highly educated at that time – not creative thinkers – to operate effectively because they were in routine jobs. The public was also less demanding then. If it took the passport-processing expert three months to complete the task, people grumbled, but they also made sure they sent the paperwork in early.

Today, however, the mood has changed. People won't wait three months for a passport. They booked the flight yesterday, leave next week, and expect immediate service. The passport office – and all the other offices of government – can't maintain that traditional buffer any longer because the public won't accept it. The passport application is handed in and completed by next week – unless it's an emergency, in which case you'll get it later today.

That leads to a new model, without buffers, as shown in Figure 7.3. Public servants are no longer confined to one area of expertise; they are expected to be broader in outlook. They are organized into teams which have a combination set of skills. They deal directly with the public and other organizations that cover similar terrain. Management is underneath that structure, in a supporting role.

Take, for example, a passport application that requires a criminal check. In the old days, our expert might send the passport application to her supervisor, who would pass it on to the requisite supervisor at the police, asking for the check. The police supervisor would kick it down to a technical-core specialist, who would carry out the work, shoot it back up, and then it would be shuffled back to the original passport expert.

That cumbersome approach has been abandoned by the best agencies. The first stage in elimination was to free the person in the passport office to call up her opposite number in the police and get the information. The second stage was to expand her responsibilities so she could call up the police data bank on her own screen and check it out herself. So we've moved from a one-way, feed-things-up-and-down model, in which the client was depersonalized and the public servant insulated, to a two-way sharing process, with

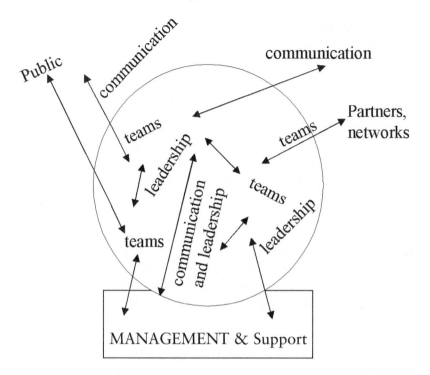

Figure 7.3 Emerging public sector organization.

teams. Not all public service agencies have taken this approach, and those that have maintained J.D. Thompson's model are having difficulty meeting customer expectations. New Brunswick's social services has moved to more intimate contact with their clients. New Zealand's social services have moved to storefront offices, where clients sit at desks with the staff. Both pay attention to personal security issues, given the sometimes angry and unpredictable responses of their clients, but they do so in a dynamic fashion.

FISHBOWLS AND OTHER EXTERNAL COMMUNICATIONS

Metropolitan Toronto's staff thrive under the freer model, operating exuberantly in a multilingual fishbowl. The media have offices near officials and prowl the hallways looking for stories. All information is public as soon as it hits the various public committees – which is much sooner than equivalent reports in higher levels of government. It's common for a reporter to call up an official and say that he'll be over in a few minutes to chat about a given issue. "The reporters are known to us by first name. They are our ears and our mouthpiece to the public," says Firoz Kara, assistant director of Corporate Planning.

Kara used to be a consultant with Canada's federal government, where there's greater insulation from the media: "It's very different here. It was quite a cultural change for me when I came from Ottawa." It's such an open, fast-paced environment that if he leaves a meeting at 10:00 p.m., he can turn on the television when he arrives home and learn the results on the late news – as can the public.

Toronto is one of the world's most multicultural centres. Its translation bureau handles the challenge of making sure communications from the civic government are understood by the populace. Since money is limited, the unit decides the main target for each communication and the appropriate languages for translation. The Italian community formed an early migration wave, for example, and most of its young people speak English, but many elders born in Italy still do not read English. So a pamphlet on day care won't be translated into Italian, while a brochure on old-age homes would be. A recent recycling brochure was distributed in 11 languages – and some other civic material is translated into as many as 18 languages. The bureau also hooks up with AT&T's language line, which provides translators in 120 languages for queries to Access Metro, the city's info/help line.

THE DISAPPEARING SILOS

For the best part of the past century, the structure of government has remained essentially unchanged. It has been organized vertically, in a traditional hierarchical arrangement: power flows from the head of state, through the cabinet minister, to the senior public servant, and down to the managers and employees. Departments are established to deal with specific areas of responsibility such as agriculture, defense, and immigration. Those departments are similarly organized with information flowing up and down through the hierarchy.

But silos are for storage. Networks are for exchange. As society becomes more complicated, many issues become increasingly horizontal. They cannot be resolved by one department of the public service without help from other departments, as well as the private, voluntary or non-profit sectors. Dealing with illegal immigrants, for example, requires cooperation among police, correctional agencies, the courts, immigration offices, taxation officials, and social insurance departments. It relies heavily on the cooperation of citizens to report illegal immigrants and on private sector businesses and individual citizens not to employ them. Cross-border coordination is also required with the immigrant's country of origin. In cases where human rights or refugee status come into play, the international community and the United Nations may become involved. All of this cannot be confined to the traditional "stovepipe" bureaucracy. Networking is needed.

Networking can be the result of a government-wide redefinition of the role of government, forging new relationships among levels of government, within government, and between government and the private sector. Or it can be an individual agency initiative to improve connections with partners or citizens. To be effective, an organization must be able to manage each of these networking relationships – and manage them well. That means scanning the environment, identifying potential stakeholders, establishing networks, and remaining involved.

It involves far more than exchanging information, responding to requests, and having civilized chats with agency heads over cocktails. An intimate, sustained, cross-agency involvement is required, at all levels of the organization. Networking is a conscious effort to "expand the envelope" to include those partners, from the ground up, from start to finish.

Our respondents each used a variety of methods to manage horizontal issues, with considerable similarities in the specific techniques and no real differences across culture, size of organization, or mandate. The techniques included interdepartmental committees, conferences, joint task forces, international agreements, memorandums of understanding (which can actually be viewed as joint mission statements), memberships in professional organizations, and liaison with interest groups.

All our well-performing organizations reach out to important constituencies. The RCMP has a series of advisory committees for communities such as aboriginals and youth, to allow two-way exchange. "We shouldn't pretend to know what a community needs without asking," says David Cleveland, director of Human Resources. Stephen Jacobi served as a special link to the business community when Richard Nottage wanted to reach out to that vital constituency for the foreign affairs and trade ministry. The message was clear: if you have any problem, just call the designated person in my office and he'll help you out. Nottage was later named New Zealander of the Year by the *National Business Review*, a leading private sector business publication, in part for that special sensitivity.

Egypt's Cabinet Information Support Centre sees itself as a channel to the world for a country that is growing economically and technologically. The centre has fought hard to make it clear that the global information society must extend beyond the G-7 countries. They attend conferences around the world and pay particular attention to sharing their advances with other countries in the developing world, notably South Africa and Malaysia. "It's not just North-South. It's South-South as well in information technology," says the centre's Ahmed Nazif.

The list of communications activities by our well-performing agencies is endless. But that's the nature of the endeavor. Communications, which our sample ranked as the third most important of our key attributes, is so broad that it even includes body-language. Managers must take care that the messages they emit through body language are consistent with the accompanying verbal messages.

Effective public service departments think about communications and networking – and the citizens they serve. They plan their communications with staff from newsletters to tailgate meetings (although they recognize serendipity can help). They are attentive to the citizens they serve, shedding the insulating barrier of old for quicker service and greater contact. Location, they know, matters. They also think about their relationships with other public, private, and not-for-profit agencies, determining and nurturing relationships which will forward their mission. For well-performing organizations, communications is the never-ending story.

CAPSULES

• Location has helped the Norwegian Petroleum Directorate in networking with the industry it regulates. For Revenue Canada, serendipity has led to a proliferation of useful internal newsletters.

- The hard part of communications is that it must be an interchange.
- A bubble chart is a useful technique for beginning a communications strategy.
- After identifying people and organizations on your bubble chart, start to define – and manage – expectations.
- One of the great mistakes that managers make is to assume people are mind readers.
- Face-to-face contact is often ideal for communications.
- Agencies must pro-actively manage their standing and reputation, like Statistics Canada.
- Regular meetings are a well-used channel of communications for our well-performing organizations, bringing people together in everything from tailgate sessions to breakfast gatherings to free-wheeling employee forums.
- Too often organizations and individuals are just dumping information. It's important, therefore, that managers divide their time among activities in a reasoned way rather than becoming an elevated switchboard clerk.
- Communications-related criticism is not necessarily a bad thing. It can be a sign that people are short of other things to complain about.
- Communications is a constant struggle to determine how frequently, what format, and to how many people.
- Some of our well-performing organizations evaluate their internal communications by staff surveys. Informal checking is also effective to determine if the intended message is being received.
- In the new model of public administration, public servants are no longer confined to one area of expertise: they are expected to be broader in outlook. They are organized into teams which have a combination of skills. They deal directly with the public and other organizations that cover similar terrain. Management is underneath that structure, in a supporting role.
- Silos are for storage. Networks are for exchange.
- All our well-performing organizations reach out to important constituencies.
- For well-performing organizations, communications is the never-ending story.

EXPLORATIONS

In our survey we asked about communications and networking: *Describe the way (both the "what" and the "how") in which your organization communicates and otherwise interacts, both internally and externally. How do you "manage" communication and relationships? What is important and what is not important in this area?*

How does your organization understand and define its place in the system of organizations of which it is one part, and how does your organization manage (in the broadest sense) its natural network? Also, how does your organization ensure that it is helpful in solving interdepartmental – horizontal – issues (issues which require the involvement of several organizations apart from your own)?

Other questions you might want to consider include:

Do you have a good understanding of who you need to communicate with, and how well you fare at it?

Would a bubble chart or its equivalent be useful for you personally? For your organization?

For the people and organizations on your bubble chart, are the expectations clear of how and when you communicate? Of what constitutes quality service?

How can you manage those expectations?

Do you have an internal communications plan?

Do you have an external communications plan?

What are the strengths and weaknesses of those plans?

CHAPTER 8

Trust

When the RCMP decided to adopt community policing in the late 1980s, it gradually realized that its command-and-control culture had to be dropped. Police organizations are traditionally authority-conscious, top-down structures. But community policing is the policing manifestation of the shift to quality control and delegation elsewhere in society. It's a bottom-up process, in which the cues are taken from external sources and the front-line officer dealing with the public needs the freedom to respond.

It depends on trust. The public must trust the front-line officers. The front-line officers must trust the public. And the front-line officers and management must trust each other, so that proper, independent action will occur.

But trust was a scarce commodity at the RCMP. The training program for managers was derided as the "Hate School," for supposedly teaching officers to hate their subordinates. Nobody trusted its graduates and the graduates didn't seem to trust their staff.

The RCMP's practice had become "When in doubt, write a regulation" as a result of a 1981 Royal Commission report. The politicians didn't trust the force and mechanisms were introduced to tightly control behavior. "We put in place policies and procedures that were so extensive they could choke a horse. You couldn't do your job without violating a policy. The safest thing was to do nothing," says Assistant Commissioner Cleve Cooper, director of community, contract, and aboriginal policing services.

Community policing had been initially viewed by management as simply a service-delivery innovation. But its introduction unexpectedly threw the entire management agenda on the table since com-

munity policing couldn't co-exist with the command-and-control
structure. To be successful externally, the RCMP had to change internally. And in order to instigate change, the RCMP had to rebuild
trust. "Mistrust is the number one impediment to bringing about
change," says Superintendent Dwight McCallum, who is in charge
of community policing services. "Command-and-control structures
build up mistrust."

We would be tempted to declare that close to a decade later the
RCMP has found trust. But we're hesitant to suggest that, because
the force itself won't. The RCMP's response to our questionnaire
stood out from all the others because it was the only one that
included sections savaging the organization. All the other agencies
spoke in one voice, answering each question with many examples
of success. The RCMP spoke in several voices, with various directorates contributing surprisingly candid thoughts, some speaking
proudly of achievements and others suggesting frankly that if the
claimed success wasn't smoke-and-mirrors, it still had yet to be
proven.

The dissenting reports, rather than reflecting a bloody organizational civil war, were in fact quite civil, indicating a healthy ability
to be open. The different directorates responding respected one
another, were seeking the same goals, and – here's the key word –
trusted each other enough to debate these issues openly and honestly in an official report to outsiders writing on organizational
effectiveness. We had come upon an organization with a long and
rich history of good performance, which was continuing to achieve
its aim while dramatically changing its operations, and indeed,
parts of its character. The result was a learning organization, open
with each other and with us, about their issues and struggles.

"Ten years ago, you would not have gotten a report like that,"
says Cooper. His boss, the man who signed the covering letter with
the report, is sanguine, despite the document's searing self-criticism.
"I'm not uncomfortable," Commissioner Philip Murray says quietly. "It's brutally honest." That attitude and his efforts to consult
and listen, through such activities as town hall meetings, has earned
him plaudits – and, yes, trust. "He is striving to be transparent. He
involves people in the process, communicating why he is taking a
position and demanding the same from subordinates," says McCallum. The curriculum at the management school, need we add, has
changed.

But, McCallum is quick to add, "there are still pockets of resistance." And the commissioner agrees: "We're not there yet. We still have pockets of resistance, who believe that you can run an organization like this by issuing orders and expecting them to be carried out. I think that's pretty naive given the expectations people have of themselves and the public have of police today. They want to play a role."

TRUST NO LONGER ASSUMED

Murray joined the RCMP in the early 1960s, before the social agitation later in that decade. Over the years, he has watched society change and, with it, the nature of his officers. He grew up at a time when patriotism and the establishment were held high. Today, folks are more cynical – even the more conservative souls that policing tends to draw. "People are suspicious of authority today. That's the environment you have to function in. A generation ago you could assume the trust was there. Today you have to earn it – and not once, but continuously," he says. "You can't just issue orders and put out internal newspapers. At every level, management must be seen as part of the solution for the rank and file."

The RCMP's internal magazine, *Pony Express*, follows that philosophy. It models itself after the top newsmagazines, trying to report on the force's activities with the openness of outside media rather than the boosterish cheerleading of many organizational publications. The intent is to build trust in the publication and, through that, readership and interest. Some senior managers wanted to continue to vet articles before they were printed but the publisher, Chief Superintendent Dawson Hovey, refuses: "If it becomes an organ of management we'll go back to where we were five years ago."

The RCMP was clogged with grievances from staff, a legacy of past mistrust. Management has been trying to deal with systemic problems – the so-called parking lot issues that burst out in the first stage of preparing the organization's mission statement. Alternate Dispute Resolution has also been embraced, to break down barriers and reach settlements more easily and with less bitterness. Getting to yes[1] has become an organizational watchword in dealing with these grievances internally and also improved community policing. The RCMP's ability to deal with conflict has been praised by Dr Mary Rowe of the Massachusetts Institute of Technology as "among the very best in North America,"[2] and by Cathy Costantino, author of *Designing Conflict Management Systems*,[3] as "state-of-the-art."

It's all part of walking the talk. Building trust by actions rather than words. And encouraging openness, honesty, and trust. Murray points to his Town Halls, where regular officers are eager to tell him what's wrong, as proof something right is happening: "They used to tell the bosses what the bosses wanted to hear. If we are to move the organization, we have to be honest with each other."

THE METAPHORS OF TRUST

We originally saw trust as a matter of safety: a trusting workplace is the opposite of a climate of fear. The survey responses provided a wide range of vivid metaphors, from "the glue that holds us together" to "the lubricant that allows the wheels to roll" to "trust is a reciprocal commodity with a limited bank balance."

Trust is a key element of organizational success and an essential component of organizational character. It spawns openness. It gives birth to learning. We all know how important trust is in our personal relationships. We are only beginning to realize its increasing importance in organizations that perform well. An early advocate, Gordon Shea,[4] wrote in a 1984 American Management Association monograph, "trust is the miracle ingredient of organizational life – a lubricant that reduces friction, a bonding agent that glues together disparate parts, a catalyst that facilitates action. No substitute – neither threat nor promise – will do the job as well."

THE ELEMENTS OF TRUST

Originally, we doubted that trust was significant enough to be a separate category in the survey. It has a place in the literature, but a small place, and it is not much talked about around the management table. We were surprised, and delighted, that our respondents highlighted trust as essential to organizational leadership. If people aren't trustworthy they shouldn't be leaders. It's that simple.

Trust ties into organizational learning. The foundation of organizational learning is that one values the truth – the organization has a total commitment to truth, which will lead to growth. In a

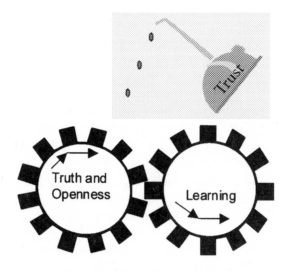

Trust lubricates

non-trusting organization – a fearful organization – people's first loyalty is protecting themselves. They believe their leaders are not trustworthy. Growth is thwarted.

Organizations cannot perform well without trust. Problems won't be spotted early; difficulties will only be recognized when they are so obvious that nobody can miss them and the energy required to deal with them has therefore escalated significantly. The cost of doing business in untrustworthy organizations soars. Undoubtedly some short-term organizational improvement can be attained by intimidation and fear. But we doubt a high level of performance can be sustained in that fashion – and certainly none of our well-performing organizations would consider that route.

In trusting climates, staff are more likely to suggest improvements. Many exemplary ideas, after all, are not immediately apparent. They need to be brought out, talked about, polished and fed. That only happens – or certainly happens more frequently – in a climate of trust. Sometimes in organizations, the emperor has no clothes and that can only be brought to the emperor's attention if the employee trusts that it will be received graciously rather than with his or her execution for daring to speak the truth. In a climate of fear, creativity and high energy hide in the closet.

Organizational trust isn't on-off – a situation of all trust or all fear – but graduated. In evaluating people, we don't completely trust them or completely distrust them. Trust is measurable along a continuum from high to low. It can also vary with the circumstances. We may trust some people in their professional lives but not their personal lives. We might trust others on only some issues or on certain occasions.

In that vein, trust can be built – as the RCMP's story shows. Once you recognize the importance of trust, you can develop strategies to enhance it. You can bring people together in certain structures to promote trust. You can change management behavior so that trust blooms. And that doesn't take a lifetime. It can be accomplished in a matter of weeks or months – years at most. One agency said that it's good we have cynics because cynics are people who basically want to believe. It's the same situation with trust. People want to trust. But they are cautious, based on their experience. The RCMP report reflected that: clearly they had developed trust, but not total agreement on the state of the organization.

THE FOUR TYPES OF TRUST

Well-performing public service agencies strive to build four different types of trust – professional, personal, political, and public. Professional trust is the degree to which you believe co-workers, subordinates, and managers are competent and committed to acting in a manner that is consistent with the mission and stated values. The absence of professional trust leads individuals to act unilaterally because they cannot rely on others. It leads to accountability systems designed to detect and punish error. It produces "directive" management styles.

The presence of professional trust is shown through delegation, clear and open communications, sharing of information, professional development, job rotations, and transformational leadership (the commitment to helping people develop). Trust is built by managers who are professionally competent, are able to manage change safely, and are concerned about employees' welfare, training, and development. It is also built by competent, motivated staff. The trust must flow in two directions: management for staff and staff for management. Two-way trust enhances both values and performance. The quality of work improves and people experience more joy in carrying that work out.

Personal trust is the degree to which one believes others are honest and caring at a personal level. Do they cheat on their travel claims, spread rumors, claim credit for work they didn't perform, or harass others? Are they ethical? Can they be relied on to produce what they promise? Without personal trust, staff become overly concerned with personal protection and covering their backsides, consuming valuable energy that would, in the presence of trust, be focused on the mission. With trust, people are more open, creative, and willing.

Political trust is the degree to which the elected government has confidence that the agency is performing competently and that its mission is compatible with the overall government agenda. A sensible direction, supported by political trust, allows a department to pursue its mission over the long term. For example, many of our respondents had long-standing mission statements that had been supported by successive governments. When political trust is lacking, there will be increased external control. The organization loses sight of its North Star, and is subject to the personal whims of short-term leaders, often parachuted in because they are trusted by the political decision-makers.

Public trust is the degree to which the public believes in the integrity of the organization and its members. Two essential prerequisites are ethical behavior and satisfactory service. No amount of advertising or baffle gab can overcome the damage when the public sees members of an agency behaving unethically or providing inferior service.

While public trust is relevant to all departments, the two Revenue Agencies in our sample (Canada and New Zealand) highlighted how important public trust is in their field. They both depend on an honor system. Taxpayers fill out their forms, remit tax, and are trusted to do so accurately. In return, for the taxpayers to act honestly, they must trust that the Revenue Department is honestly and competently managed.

TRUST AND SOCIAL FACTORS

In some societies, organizational trust is driven by social or cultural norms. "Egyptians start by trusting and only do the opposite if necessary. It's built in: trust comes as an input. You have to keep the trust," says Ahmed Nazif. His Cabinet Support Centre ensures that trust is maintained. When departments forward their monthly performance statements, for example, it is assumed the self-assessments are honest. Nobody second-guesses, them even though big bucks are disbursed through the incentive system. "You take the person's word for it and at the end of a quarter check back. If he keeps saying they've been achieving 80 per cent of target instead of 50 per cent, at some point you'll find out," he notes. The managers monitor globally, rather than distrustfully scrutinizing smaller actions.

Norwegian society's muted class distinctions and heightened sense of equality provides a basis for greater trust. The nation's social classes are more compressed than in other countries, without the huge gaps between rich and poor. Even the monarch has been called the "People's King," to reflect the fact he can talk with anyone and is monarch of a country of equals. Those aspects of Norwegian culture translate into the workplace. Communications are easier and trust higher, because social distance is reduced. By law, labor unions are also represented on all boards, creating an opportunity for openness and trust.

As in Egypt, the Norwegian Petroleum Directorate trusts people to act properly unless proven otherwise. That applies to the companies it regulates. Instead of devising strict control measures, the organization relies on trusting relationships, treating the operators as friends rather than the enemy. "If you look to them as an enemy, you will try to control. If it's a friend, you can discuss and work together. You can trust what he tells you. All of regulation is based on trust," says Paul Bang, head of strategic planning.

Muskogee Veterans Benefits spent time consciously thinking of methods to improve trust. One vehicle was the new flextime policy. Management announced it would trust employees to provide eight hours of work at any point during the 6 a.m. to 6 p.m. time span, without any checking. In fact, management went further, telling staff that they would be allowed to judge on bad weather days whether to come in late or leave early. "The message was: we trust you to be responsible," says Vicky Wilcoxen, the Total Quality Control co-ordinator.

Statistics Canada also spends a lot of time pondering trust. Its statistics must be trusted for the organization to survive. Internally, its managers must also be trusted by staff. Those managers realized that they would face a crucial test with the corporate assignments rotational program. The rules guaranteed that anyone with four years in their current post could swap jobs, even if their boss felt they couldn't be spared. Management realized that if some divisions quietly subverted the policy, trust for management in general would be eroded. "You have to watch what you put in place. Can we all live with it?" Eve Simpson says.

Karen Mann, deputy minister of New Brunswick Human Resources Development, remembers that when the minister and deputy minister of social services from another jurisdiction visited their offices the duo expressed surprise that they were allowed to wander around unescorted and able to talk, unfiltered, with staff. Mann couldn't imagine acting any differently, however: "You have to trust people if they are going to trust you."

Mann feels that trust is built up in bad times as well. A crucial test was how she handled the re-engineering of her department, in which some people lost their jobs and others had to assume new tasks. She knew employees would focus intently on the fairness and equity of management's decisions. "The importance of trust cannot be underestimated in this situation, because it is now becoming apparent that for many employees their level of commitment to the new organization is significantly influenced by their perception of how the department treated those employees who lost positions and accepted early retirement during the transformation," she notes.

Limits to trust exist, sometimes deliberately developed by organizations and in other cases externally imposed or stirred up by human nature. The Northwest Territories Workers' Compensation Board incorporated enhanced computer system safeguards in a recent systems conversion. A rare case of staff member misappropriating funds resulted in other staff feeling shocked and betrayed, and led the board to develop a strategy to cover fraud by staff, claimants, employers, and suppliers.

All our agencies face audits to ensure financial integrity, even though that is a limit on trust. Similarly, legislative and policy requirements must be met. And of course, cynicism – internal and external – can limit trust. Staff who are unmotivated, fit poorly with organizational values, or lack commitment to the mission can also reduce organizational trust.

Although fear is the enemy of trust, a little organizational discomfort can be healthy. Well-performing organizations ensure that staff feel anxious about non-performance or complacency. Jack Welch urges managers to make clear to employees the marked difference between doing well and doing less well. That introduces fear: people, after all, don't want to be reminded of their short-comings. But organizational trust does not mean staff must be promised eternal love. It simply means that they can count on leaders acting as they say they will.

Indeed, Jack Welch warns General Electric's employees that their unit will be sold off if it doesn't perform well. That's about as frightening a statement that one can hear from a boss. But it actually enhances trust because Jack Welch follows through. His staff may not like his warning but they know he is a man of integrity and will carry out his pledge. Welch shows that you can offer staff bad news, as long as you act honestly and truthfully, and assist them through the difficult transitions.

Building Trust

In our sample, trust was not left to grow on its own but deliberately fostered. Specific actions some of our respondents have taken include:

- Having a strategy to create and develop trust.
- Listening to staff. Surveys are employed in Denmark, Singapore, America, Canada, and Egypt to provide insight into the degree of trust and areas to improve on. In Denmark, the surveys assess confidence in management as a whole and the specific divisional head.
- Developing staff. The U.S. Defense Mapping Agency, which operates in a highly specialized field, builds professional trust through a cartographic certification program modeled after professional engineering certification. It is a three-stage process assessing past performance, technical abilities, and leadership. The process includes peer review. Once certified, employees are promoted and given more trust and responsibility.
- Performance measurement and audits. "Staff do not see these as a lack of trust, but rather a necessary check to instill greater public trust in the Central Provident Fund Board," writes planning officer Celine Tan.
- Building teams and delegating. Together, these show that people are trusted to be responsible for themselves. Muskogee veterans benefits observes: "It is a contradiction in terms to say you have an empowered, team-based organization, but you do not rank

'trust' as one of your top areas of importance. Without trust you revert back to an organization with too much control and supervision, and a workforce that feels monitored and restricted."

- Recognizing staff accomplishments and valuing them, through the wide variety of methods we've mentioned earlier.
- Sharing information. Muskogee veterans benefits now trusts employees with information which was historically reserved for senior management. They trust it will be used to achieve the mission, and not used in a manner that would be detrimental to the service.
- Thinking about how to maintain or restore trust during and after major change. In 1992, Revenue Canada integrated the two arms of its department: Taxation and Customs and Excise. The new organization focused on sensitivity to employees needs, continuous learning, team work, humor, communications, and client satisfaction. By 1995, with three years of effort concentrated on understanding and trust, the trust and satisfaction levels had returned to their previous high levels.
- Making trust a leadership function. Statistics Canada advises: "Employees develop a sense of trust in an organization not by listening to senior management espouse high-minded principles but rather by observing the actions and decisions of these managers. In particular they watch to see whether senior management keeps its promises even in the face of competing priorities."
- U.S. Armaments Research uses trust as a basis for partnering activities with the union, for which it has received a best practice award. They openly share good and bad information as soon as possible. The Commanding General hosts open forums with a combination of live audience and phone-ins.
- The National Library of Canada recognizes that "Gatherings of the Clan" are important "to build a personal sense of community and a foundation of trust that carries over into working relationships." Running through the replies, whether from closely knit societies or not, was a belief that relationships built outside the workplace contributed to trust within the organization. In this age of decreased commitment by governments to employment security, and an increasingly mobile workforce, our respondents still maintained a sense of belonging and loyalty to the organization.

COMMITTING TO OPENNESS

The traditional, hierarchical, authoritarian nature of public service agencies has not encouraged individuals to recognize, admit to, and learn from failures. The well-performing organizations in our sample are different: they have established a climate of openness and support improved performance through truth and learning.

Few of us like to admit our mistakes. It's more comforting to deny, suppress the evidence, and hire "spin doctors" to whitewash the situation. It's hard to speak the truth, particularly in organizational cultures where the custom has been to shoot the messenger. Interestingly, most of us initially joined our agency with a personal commitment to truth, honesty, and openness. But too often we found in traditional bureaucracies that those were counterproductive values. They were detrimental to our careers.

It can be difficult to shift from a closed organization to an open one – as the RCMP's story demonstrates. It's not that people are corrupt and don't want openness. It's simply that they find it difficult to forsake secrecy, to let go of the old practices. At the same time, the benefits of openness can show up quickly. A high degree of openness with the media, for example, provides a quick return. The media trust and understand the organization better, and more positive coverage results. Similarly, when you work openly with partners on your bubble chart, trust makes it easier to achieve consensus on what can and can't be accomplished. If you don't open the books on your shop, people will always assume you are capable of accomplishing more and that you are just dragging your feet.

All our well-performing organizations stressed the importance of being tolerant of mistakes. The Norwegian Petroleum Directorate was typical: "There should be room for mistakes in any organization and the experience gained by making those mistakes should be used to advantage rather than to punish creative and proficient staff."

Openness permits organizational learning, a concept popularized recently by Peter Senge[5] in *The Fifth Discipline* but actually built on Chris Argyris'[6] work of a quarter century ago. In learning organizations, everybody is constantly improving, staff are encouraged to try new ways of thinking, and a collective vision of creating the best has been set loose.

Canadian sprinter Donovan Bailey exemplifies that spirit. Shortly after he won the gold medal for running 100 meters in world-record time at the 1996 Atlanta Olympics, he told reporters: "My coach and I reviewed the race. There are things that I can improve on. I have not yet run my best race." Bailey went on to beat the 200 meter champion in a 150 meter match race for bragging rights as the "world's fastest man". He was less than gracious toward the person he defeated, but he subsequently apologized and acknowledged he could improve his interpersonal skills as well as his running. That attitude for continuous improvement is exactly what Jac Fitz-Eng of the Saratoga Institute says successful organizations must take to heart: "They aren't content with doing it great; they're committed to doing it better."[7]

LEARNING ORGANIZATIONS

Learning organizations must overcome the defenses that inhibit effectiveness and greater levels of awareness and honesty. Ralph Heintzman, in a report by the Canadian Centre for Management Development,[8] pointed out that organizational learning "begins with the individual because only individuals can learn. But individual learning can be promoted and supported by an organizational culture in which individuals are encouraged by all possible means to participate in a continuous process of learning and growth."

Heintzman stressed the difference between learning and training. "Training implies that something already known is transferred to someone else, whereas learning implies a process of self-directed exploration and discovery, in search of something not yet known. This distinction is reflected in current trends in training, which is evolving rapidly towards greater emphasis on internally motivated learning related to the immediate needs of the workplace," he states.

Our well-performing organizations have taken learning to heart. Different formal models were used. Muskogee Veterans Benefits had applied Total Quality Management. They benchmarked against standards set nationally and against their own performance in the past. Employee-managed teams compared themselves to each other and to teams at other geographical locations. They were always stretching to find the best way of extending their capabilities.

New Zealand's Ministry of Foreign Affairs and Trade stresses the individual's responsibility for improvement. Dialogue is crucial, sharing insights. Exit interviews are an important learning oppor-

tunity, used to ferret out what departing employees consider wrong
with the organization and how it can be improved.

Almost all of our survey respondents had built a network of con-
tacts with similar agencies and private sector companies, both within their country and internationally. Benchmarking was widespread
but our agencies don't mindlessly adopt successful techniques from
other jurisdictions. They analyse innovations and judge whether
those would work within the unique context of their agency.

Some establish relationships with consulting groups which scan
the environment for relevant ideas. Executive interchange ideas and
"visiting scholars" sprinkle in the insights of outsiders.

The agencies reported several impediments to learning. Organizations must have the proper information systems for learning to
occur. The systems must also be open and accessible to all. Financial resources must be available. And, of course, staff must be willing to learn.

In his early days in corrections, long before he heard of Senge or
Argyris, Paul remembers falling into a somewhat public confronta-
tion with a long-time prison guard. As others watched them debate,
the veteran, Sully, thought he had the irrefutable position: "Paul,
I've got 21 years experience in this and you only have 3. Now who
do you think knows more?" Being young, brash and not too politically astute at the time, Paul replied: "Well Sully, I think I do,
because you basically have 1 year's experience that you've repeated
21 times, and I've spent 3 years learning. So I've got 3 years' experience and you've got 1."

Sully was a good man and he had done a good job – operating in
a system where learning was not all that necessary for most of his
career. But even then, in the mid-1970s, and certainly now, late into
the 1990s, you cannot survive in the correctional environment, or
in any public-service environment, without continuous learning.
And that takes character. The desire to learn, to become better, is a
personality characteristic needed in public service: staff must want
to learn and to perform their job as well as possible.

Finally, we have to stress again that fear and lack of trust are an
impediment to learning. Indeed, laboratory experiments show that
when fear is induced, learning plunges. In fact, you forget what you
learned in the past, as well as failing to learn new material. So organizations must create a climate of trust, openness, and calmness for
learning to take place.

Styles of Learning

Some new models of learning blur the boundaries between work and learning, between individual learning and organizational learning. All were in use, depending on the need, in our sample.

Experiential learning includes simulations, role-playing, games, exercises, team-building, outward-bound activity, and feedback. It also involves interactive, peer-based learning, on-site visits, and observing others.

Active learning takes experiential learning a step further, as a "real-use" exercise is attached to the training. The group prepares a report on a specific issue or work problem, which becomes part of the organization's process. For example, the group might look at a particularly difficult record-keeping issue or could visit another site to benchmark it and report on how to improve.

Action learning is another step along the continuum. Participants become responsible for implementing a solution to a problem, not just studying and reporting it.

Adult-learning principles are also increasingly replacing traditional classroom lectures, since staff like to learn this way. Teachers are practitioners rather than professional educators. They first describe the learning, then model it, then provide the learners with practice and feedback. The learners share their own workplace experiences with their fellow learners. They develop a plan to use the newly learned ideas back on the job and follow-up occurs.

EARTHQUAKE PROTECTION

To cope with earthquakes, a New Zealand group has developed an engineering technique that rests buildings on rubber-and-steel bearings that in turn rest on cement pillars that reach into the bedrock. Called "base isolators," they act like shock absorbers on a car, isolating the building from most of the ground movement during an earthquake. In a similar way, the aim and character of an organization provide protection from the earthquakes of economics, the hurricanes of politics, and the tornadoes of interpersonal relations. The organizations are rock solid, thanks to the first two pillars of public management.

In the event of The Big One, an earthquake of 8.5 or more on the

Richter scale, the base-isolator technique is designed to protect the people but the building may have to be demolished and rebuilt. So too with the public service, when the base isolators of aim and character are in place. Some of our respondents had aim and character that had been stable for over a century. Others had undergone recent massive changes. But the people were protected, and they rebuilt, adjusting to the new terrain and environment. They executed well, managing change, which is our third pillar.

CAPSULES

- Trust is a key element of organizational success and an essential component of organizational character. It spawns openness. It gives birth to learning.
- Trust is closely related to its opposite, fear.
- The cost level of untrustworthy organizations soars as problems are spotted late. Innovation is hampered because people are afraid to voice new or contrary ideas.
- Once you recognize the importance of trust, you can develop strategies to enhance it.
- Building trust begins with creating a culture based on shared values. The second step is for leadership to act in accordance with the new values and vision. The third step is to build relationships based on honesty, integrity and genuine concern for others.
- The organization's reward system must encourage high levels of trust by rewarding trustful behavior and punishing untrustworthy behavior.
- Well-performing public service agencies work to build four different types of trust – professional, personal, political, and public.
- In some societies, organizational trust is driven by social factors, such as Egypt's belief that people are trustworthy unless proven otherwise and Norway's social equality.
- Well-performing organizations develop trust strategies. They listen to staff and develop staff professionally so they will be more trustworthy. They use performance measures and audits to display trustworthiness. They empower staff and recognize accomplishments.
- Limits to trust exist, including controls, audits, and cynicism.

- A little organizational discomfort can be a healthy thing: well-performing organizations ensure that the staff feel anxious about non-performance and complacency.
- The traditional, hierarchical, authoritarian nature of public service agencies has not encouraged individuals to recognize, admit, and learn from failures. The well-performing organizations in our sample are different: they have established a climate of openness and support improved performance through truth and learning.
- The Norwegian Petroleum Directorate speaks for others when it says: "There should be room for mistakes in any organization and the experience gained by making those mistakes should be used to advantage rather than to punish creative and proficient staff."
- In learning organizations, everybody is constantly improving, people are encouraged to try new ways of thinking, and a collective vision of creating the best has been set loose.
- Organizational learning begins with the individual because only individuals can learn.
- Organizations must have the proper information systems for learning to occur. The systems must also be open and accessible to all. Financial resources must be available. And, of course, people must be willing to learn.
- Fear and lack of trust are an impediment to learning.
- Aim and character are base isolators, protecting organizations from the earthquakes of economics, the hurricanes of politics, and the tornadoes of interpersonal relations. They allow organizations to execute change.

EXPLORATIONS

In our survey we asked: *How would you describe your organization in terms of being transparent, open, sharing, committed to the truth and operating in a mode of learning from its own experiences (good and bad) and from the experience of others?*

Describe the role of trust in the daily life of your organization. To what extent is trust in leaders (personal trust, professional trust) important to your organization? How would you know whether it is there, and to what degree it is there? Also, how important is it in your organization that leaders and managers trust each other, as

well as trust the employees? Are there limits to trust? If so, is it pos-
sible to define those limits within your organization?

Other questions you may want to consider include:

Can you trust others in your organization?

Can they trust you?

Can you speak the truth to those in power?

Looking at the four types of trust – professional, personal, political, and public – how well is your organization doing?

What is undermining each kind of trust?

What can be done to build more trust?

How open is the organization?

What can be done to improve openness?

Is yours a learning organization?

Are you learning, developing, growing professionally?

How can the organization better contribute to learning, developing, and improving?

Five Centuries ago, Machiavelli said "It is better to be feared than to be loved." Is that true today, or is it better to be trusted than to be feared?

Execution

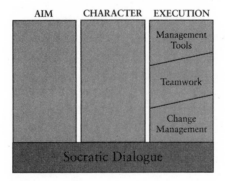

CHAPTER 9

Management Tools

It started with TQM (Total Quality Management). Next a layer of teams was added. Then came a dash of process reengineering. And throughout, as Muskogee's Veterans Benefits office aimed to become a prototype of government effectiveness, other management tools, from incentives to training to improved communications, were applied as needed. "We kept looking at what is out there to help us grow," says Vicky Wilcoxen, the Total Quality Control co-ordinator. "While we think we're doing well, we're not in Nirvana yet."

The Muskogee regional office is one of the largest in the U.S. Veterans Benefits Administration, administering a full-range of compensation, pension, vocational rehabilitation and home loans for veterans and their families in the state of Oklahoma, as well as education benefits for 33 per cent of the nation's veterans and on-the-job training for about 10,000 veterans.

Pressured by politicians for better delivery of services at less cost, and by staff for an improved work environment, the agency set out in 1991 to respond. It began with Total Quality Management, despite the nay-sayers and those suggesting management was succumbing to the flavor of the month. It decided on the 7-step process popularized by Florida Power and Light. Over the next 24 months, all employees received orientation in TQM principles, 50 per cent had received team member training, and 19 teams developed quality measures.

But frustration was building. The 7-step process can be slow and the results to that point had been modest. Looking to speed up the process, somebody suggested experimenting with employee-

managed teams, which seemed a logical extension of the TQM appa-
ratus. Two processing teams were created and within three months
dramatic cycle-time improvements had been achieved by using data
analysis, brainstorming, and consensus. "Teams could take action
quickly," notes Wilcoxen. "They took control of their own work
and could make decisions in a day that used to take six months. If
they made a mistake they could see it and fix it quickly."

The agency dubbed the combined technique "TQM-based
Employee-Managed Teams." Within six months, half the staff was
immersed in the new quality improvement culture, up from only 10
per cent before the two management tools were fused. Within a
year, the agency had achieved almost 100 per cent participation,
with 28 employee-managed teams meeting weekly under TQM
guidelines.

APPLYING MORE TOOLS

At the same time, the agency started to feed in some of the National Performance Review's ideas, notably increased customer focus,
empowerment, and improved diversity. For decades, the international standard in government had been one supervisor for each
five to seven subordinates, which automatically builds a hierarchy.
When Vice President Al Gore, who headed the National Performance Review, called for a supervisor-to-employee ratio in government of 1 to 15, Muskogee, true to its insistence on becoming a
prototype, far surpassed this goal, achieving a 1 to 40 level.

Doing so involved cutting 27 supervisory positions, which were
proving a barrier to the full functioning of employee teams anyway,
since the supervisors still wanted to manage. Now, coaching is the
norm. Teams are told to work out problems themselves; when
stymied, they can go to the coach for advice. Only if that fails to
produce a solution should they approach the supervisory level. For
the former supervisors who remained with the agency as coaches,
Wilcoxen notes that "it was traumatic in the beginning. But they
learned people treated them with respect not because of their
authority but because of their knowledge and skills. So they are
now validated in a different way."

Obsessed with customer service, the various teams began a
"Writing for Real People" offensive to re-jig the foggy forms they

were asking people to complete. The new material employs clear language, highlights important topics through headings, and keeps extraneous figures to a minimum. Veterans want to know from the unit how much they are going to receive and why. The letters now tell them that, directly, without confusing bureaucratic gobbledygook. The new wording was tested on focus groups of veterans to ensure that the change was truly progress, not just a case of doing things differently.

As the staff studied re-engineering, they realized it presented some benefits. They had improved internal processes. But what about starting from scratch in certain areas? What exactly needs to be in a disability delivery process? How would you construct it for maximum effectiveness? That search is continuing.

Muskogee has a Quality Council to develop policy, composed of various team leaders and supervisors (excluding, as we have mentioned, the overall director). It has a range of incentive programs. Training is extensive, including lunch-and-learn sessions in which the outpourings of prominent management gurus are grappled with. Whatever can help, the agency integrates with the existing operations, while maintaining the successful elements from the past.

The results have been spectacular. Claim processing times were reduced by 30 to 70 per cent. Morale shot up. Sick leave plummeted. Muskogee teams have been asked to visit other Veterans Benefits offices to help improve performance. Private sector firms invite them to deliver training.

Nothing indicates their success better than the time frame they developed for processing widows' pension claims. Having heard about the hardship faced by those who lose a spouse, the team decided to redefine service standards. Pension claims that come by mail with full documentation are now turned around in just one day from receipt. If a widow visits personally, she is told within an hour what her benefit will be and when she will receive it.

Those full-documentation claims account for half the cases. But the Muskogee office has picked up the pace on the other half as well. When documents are missing, instead of writing back the staff member calls directly to speed the process. While the U.S. veterans benefits standard calls for such claims to take, on average, 44 days to process, at Muskogee the employee-managed teams have whittled it down to from 17 to 24 days.

The Muskogee experience illustrates the importance of the selection and use of the right management tools.

SELECTING THE RIGHT TOOL

Many organizations, as in the Kliban cartoon above, have a good product and a hard working staff. But their implementation is off. Noble goals and sincere people fail because the execution is poor: they implement ineffectively or in a fashion that actually makes things worse.

Our well-performing organizations are adept at execution. It starts, as in the cartoon, with the right product (aim) then adds committed, hard-working staff (character). The Muskogee Veterans Benefit office, for example, had a comprehensive package that met veterans needs, but their execution, their delivery, was poor. To improve, they sought out and carefully selected better management tools. The agency wasn't transfixed by one technique, whatever its luster. When problems arose, new tools that seemed to hold promise were tested. Tools that showed effectiveness were used thoroughly.

No trade pays as little attention to its tools as management. There are no specifications, no standards, no guarantees, no warranties. Too often, the manager's tool box is filled with rusty junk. It's hard to imagine an airline pilot who still uses the compass his father gave him when he was in Boy Scouts. Yet many managers still use the management techniques they learned 30 years ago.

At the other extreme, some managers purchase new tools and eagerly apply them without any thought to their effect. They seem smitten by a virus that compels them to stock their tool box with sleek new gadgets that are little more than a reminder of the most recent management craze. In the last 15 years an infectious fadishness has arisen, especially in North America, with managers and consultants embracing each new management buzzword. The symptoms of this potent, recurring virus are an initial flush of excitement for the new theory followed by a lapse in enthusiasm, fatigue, and depression, which leads to the abandonment of the fad just as a new one springs to life and attacks the weakened immune system.

To inoculate managers, a new vaccine is on the market: books that deride management fads. The Dilbert series of cartoons and books are the most popular, if rather feeble, solution. But two other books offer some sensible cynicism about the malady: Richard Tanner Pascal's *Managing on the Edge*,[1] and Eileen Shapiro's *Fad Surfing in the Boardroom*.[2] Shapiro pens some hilarious definitions of the latest trends in management, including this pointed description of fad-surfing: "The practice of riding the crest of the latest management panacea and then paddling out again just in time to ride the next one; always absorbing for managers and lucrative for consultants; frequently disastrous for organizations."

Our well-performing organizations avoid such disasters. They are well-performing in part because they are selective about management tools. If they employ a recent management tool they build on experience, rather than accepting things without question. Muskogee applied TQM and self-managed teams after some of the dangers of those approaches had been illuminated by other organizations. Our sample knows that management tools developed in the private sector must be modified to both the public sector in general and the specific agency in particular. When they apply a technique, they also apply common sense.

PROCRUSTES, HAMMER, AND CHAMPY

A management tool box should be full with a variety of implements. Managers have to be able to use them all, like any top tradesperson. They must assess the new tools appearing on the market and obtain the appropriate ones.

Too many management tools are being marketed flamboyantly as the universal solution to all your problems – no matter what those problems. Such tools tend to be solution-oriented rather than problem-oriented, designed to secure conformity at any cost, giving them a Procrustean flavour. (Procrustes was a giant in Greek mythology who seized travelers, tied them to a bedstead, and either stretched them or amputated their legs to make them fit it.) Solution-oriented approaches assume the same answer will work everywhere. But every organization has its own unique conditions and problems. It is best to start by recognizing these and working to find applicable solutions, rather than following Procrustes.

Muskogee Veterans Benefits achieved some success with TQM, but only after they modified the approach to fit their needs. Interestingly, the agency had started with the Florida Power and Light program, shortly after that utility, in 1989, became the first U.S. company to win Japan's coveted Deming Prize. But many of the rigidly applied "quality" techniques that led to the utility being honored produced trouble in the years ahead. Eventually Florida Light backed off considerably from its former approach, balancing ideas from the Quality movement with those from many other sources.

It's worth remembering that TQM was originally designed for the private sector. While it can be applied to the public sector as well, it was originally intended for organizations pursuing customers in a competitive market environment for the purpose of maximizing profit and promoting organizational expansion and survival. Not all those concerns are the public sector's concerns and Total Quality can't be transferred intact from the private to public sector. Each element of TQM must be carefully evaluated to determine if and how it fits with the requirements not just of the public sector but also of the various parts of the particular agency – and how it might be adapted to them. The elements that seem most useful – and our well-performing organizations have employed them – are continuous improvement, customer focus, business process analysis, measurement, employee involvement and recognition, teamwork, and training. Each, in effect, are management tools in their own right that skilled modern managers will apply when appropriate. TQM is a process of bundling them together, to be used at the same time.

Reengineering has been the most talked-about fad of the 90s. However, the only thing new about reengineering is the hype. As substance, it traces back a long time in management history. The hype is an outgrowth of two American consultants, Michael Hammer and James Champy,[3] who championed the technique with all sorts of extraordinary claims. They would have you believe that reengineering is the most important management technique since Adam Smith wrote *The Wealth of Nations*. They advise that "reengineering means starting all over, starting from scratch" and warn that managers who apply it "must abandon all the organizational and operational principles and procedures they are now using and create entirely new ones." Reengineering, then, is not a hammer or saw; it's a grenade.

Hammer and Champy defined reengineering as "the fundamental rethinking and radical redesign of business processes to achieve dramatic improvements in critical, contemporary measures of performance, such as cost, quality, service and speed." Stripping away the inflationary adjectives, we find little more than a proposal to reconsider and redesign business processes in order to improve quality, service, speed, and productivity.

And that isn't terribly new. One of the earliest and most successful full-scale efforts in business process improvement took place at the U.S. Bureau of the Census in the late 1930s. The objectives were quality, service, speed, and productivity!

Of course, Hammer and Champy would disagree with this historical comparison. They contend that reengineering and continuous improvement differ – you guessed it – fundamentally. Quality improvement, the inferior path, seeks only "steady, incremental improvement" to existing processes. Reengineering, the robust alternative, "seeks breakthroughs, not by enhancing existing processes but by discarding them and replacing them with entirely new ones."

That assertion is specious at best and dangerous at worst. It is specious because previous approaches to business process improvement always included the search for breakthrough or quantum improvements where achievable. It is dangerous because in limiting their perspective to breakthrough attainments in process improvement, and by advocating certain tools for that job, Hammer and Champy propose, to use their own terminology, a radical narrowing of the managerial outlook and risk taking us back a generation or two in management practice.[4]

THE DIALECT OF MANAGEMENT

To explain that danger, it's helpful to situate reengineering in the wider historical perspective. At the risk of over-simplification, the history of management theory this century has been a tension and alternation between two perspectives or impulses. The story begins with Frederick Taylor, the American businessman who codified the best practices of advanced industrial management. He analysed work processes and developed the principles of what he termed "scientific management." To achieve excellence, he recommended breaking the industrial process down into its smallest components. Those individual tasks and sub-tasks could be assigned to workers whose actions were carefully controlled to ensure they performed their own part in the process faithfully and economically, as scientifically managed.

That was a powerful new way of seeing the world which contributed enormously to building up industrial enterprise in the first half of the century. Taylor was not very skilled interpersonally, however, and Taylorism, as practiced by others over time, tended to be terribly technological and to neglect the human side of organizational life. As a result, a reaction occurred.

Beginning in the 1930s, and gathering steam in the 1940s and 1950s, a new "human relations" school evolved, especially in the United States, that challenged scientific management and re-emphasized the human dimensions of organizations. Shaped by writers like Abraham Maslow, Douglas MacGregor, Kurt Lewin, and Frederick Herzberg, this approach offered an array of new management tools that emphasized the human element in organizational life, such as leadership, communication, and employee participation.

Some writers argue that the whole history of management thought and prevailing practice should be viewed as a cyclical alternation between these two schools of thought: production techniques or technology and human relations. Some even suggest the alternations between the two waves can be related to the economic climate. Certainly the cycle has continued in the post-war era, with the strengthened engineering instinct of the war giving way to T-Groups and other human relations ideas in the 1950s. The 1960s saw the new structural school of management and "rational" management systems emerge, such as Management by Objectives and Planning Programming Budgeting Systems, better known as PPBS. In the 1970s and 1980s, the organizational development school, led by writers like Warren Bennis, Edgar Schein, and Chris Argyris, returned us to thinking about such human variables as leadership, values, organizational climate, and organizational culture. Two sets of authors, Blake and Mouton with their *Managerial Grid*, and Hersey and Blanchard with *Situational Leadership*, recognized the split and advocated combining both schools.

It was to be expected that the 1990s would witness a resurgence of the technological approach to management – and process improvement and re-engineering certainly fit the bill. Re-engineers nod occasionally in the direction of the other school, mentioning empowerment, values, coaching, leadership, and education. But that reference is limited, as if they felt it necessary to genuflect in that direction even though in reality such matters were far from the center of their genuine concern. Their unmistakable enthusiasm is reserved for information technology and its limitless capacity to generate reengineering. That unbridled enthusiasm, interestingly, is in striking contrast to Edward Deming, the father of the quality movement, who repeatedly warned against the illusion that an "expansion of computers" would solve the failures of management.

Hammer and Champy's reverence for information technology is the clear giveaway that reengineering is Frederick Taylor's scientific management reborn and remodeled for the 1990s. Taylor, of course, tried to achieve his goal by breaking down tasks while reengineering attempts to knit tasks together into processes. But the underlying spirit is the same.

Reengineering also portrays a curiously static view of organizations. Because of the elaborate reengineering methodology, Hammer and Champy seem to expect the organization to "refreeze" again, after reengineering has transpired. That is a very old approach to managing change and is an uncanny echo of Frederick Taylor and Henry Ford's search for the "one best way" of organizing manufacturing processes.

That belief overlooks the vital insight that Joseph Juran absorbed at Western Electric as early as the 1920s: business process improvement should occur continuously and unceasingly, and the processes within organizations should be arranged to allow that to occur. It is dangerous to ignore that central wisdom of continuous improvement in favor of fits and starts. Things are changing too rapidly for that to work.

For that reason, reengineering is a step backward in our understanding and practice of good management. But the greatest step backward is its advocates' obvious lack of interest or real attention to the human side of management and organizational life. This absence must be corrected by those who embrace their approach. If it is applied, as many now urge, in the public sector, where people and character are so important, it could greatly impoverish the caliber of leadership in the public sector. There are some obvious advantages to reengineering, if it is taken with a grain of salt and adapted to the needs of the individual organizations. But used in its pure form, without those cautions, it can be destructive. Fortunately, the grenade is a tool not often reached for in the effective public manager's toolbox.

THE WELL-PERFORMING TOOLBOX

Our well-performing organizations draw freely and liberally from both management streams. They have a large tool box, stuffed with people management skills, process analysis, planning analysis, coaching, mentoring, rewards and punishment, budgeting systems, communications strategies, trend analysis, and elements of TQM. All of this is rooted in a continuous learning/continuous improvement mindset.

Out of the half-dozen TQM users, none rigidly followed Deming's 14 points. They adapted and finessed. Reengineering was only used by a few from our sample – it didn't meet most needs. Reengineering blows things up and starts all over again. Well-performing organizations generally don't need to take that avenue because much is right with the agency. Muskogee did apply it in some areas, however, and New Brunswick Human Resources Development, which was attempting revolutionary change, picked reengineering as a logical tool. Both agencies are remarkably strong on people skills, so they modified reengineering, to eliminate its downside.

Our well-performing agencies don't succumb to fanaticism in applying management tools. These are tools to be used, not Gods to be worshipped. The managers read widely, understand what is available, and try to fit the tool to the task. They also know when to discard a tool.

Although not fanatics, they are thorough. That mirrors what Jac Fitz-Eng has found in the private sector: "The best companies make long-term commitments; they're not into the program-of-the-month syndrome. It's not 'quality' this month and 'benchmarking' the next month and 'reengineering' the month after that. If they go into 'quality' they go all the way. If they get into benchmarking, they make the commitment to learn how to do it right. And they follow through."[5]

Our findings are also remarkably consistent with those of Christopher Pollitt,[6] who studied a sample of public sector organizations in the United Kingdom and the United States. Pollitt focused on the impact of six management tools: decentralized budgeting, performance indicators, performance-related pay, standards, contractualization, and evaluation. He found none of the six was particularly effective for the entire sample. "The problem is not how to apply a magic set of management techniques right across the public sector; it is much more a question of seeking, in each separate case, a match of function, form and culture."

Each public service agency needs toolmakers – people who observe, think and ask questions, and then design and customize the proper management tools for their organization. Most importantly, each of us is one of the tools in the tool box. We are responsible for developing ourselves, for staying sharp.

A professional golfer we know uses only three clubs in recreational matches – a driver, seven-iron, and putter – instead of the full tool-chest of 14 clubs. With his skill level, and those golfing tools, he can keep up with most golfers. But he cannot keep up with other professional golfers. Similarly, a public service manager who uses only the few management tools that were handed to him when he first joined the organization might have been able to succeed in the more recreational climate of the past. Now, however, a full, updated tool chest is needed. At the same time, those tools shouldn't be used because they are the buzz of the moment; they should be used because they solve the problem of the moment. One of the secrets of sustained success is having a process to assess the task and the tools available, and then making sensible choices.

CAPSULES

- The quest for management tools is summed up by Vicky Wilcoxen and the Muskogee regional office of Veterans Benefits: "We keep looking at what is out there to help us grow. While we think we're doing well, we're not in Nirvana yet."
- The well-performing agencies are very careful in selecting their management tools. They aren't transfixed by one technique,

whatever its lustre. When problems arise, new tools that seem to hold promise are tested. Tools that show promise are used effectively.

- No trade pays as little attention to its tools as management. There are no specifications, no standards, no guarantees, no warranties.

- A management tool box should be jammed with a variety of implements. Managers have to be able to use them all, like any top tradesperson.

- Too many management tools are being marketed as the universal solution to all your problems – no matter what those problems. Indeed, the tools tend to be solution-oriented rather than problem-oriented, with predictable Procrustean results.

- Each element of TQM must be carefully evaluated to determine if and how it fits with the requirements not just of the public sector but of the various parts of the public sector – and how it might be adapted to them. The elements that seem most useful – and our well-performing organizations have employed them – are continuous improvement, customer focus, business process analysis, measurement, employee involvement, and recognition, teamwork, and training.

- The only thing new about reengineering is the hype. In substance, it can be traced back a long time in management history.

- Reengineering unfortunately overlooks the vital insight that Joseph Juran absorbed at Western Electric as early as the 1920s: business process improvement should occur continuously and unceasingly, and the processes within organizations should be arranged to allow that to occur.

- The greatest step backward in reengineering is the obvious lack of interest or real attention to the human side of management and organizational life. This absence must be corrected by those who embrace that approach or it could greatly impoverish the caliber of leadership in the public sector as well as in the private sector.

- Our well-performing organizations borrowed freely and liberally from both management strands. They had a large tool box, stuffed with people management skills, process analysis, planning analysis, coaching, mentoring, rewards and punishment, budgeting systems, communications strategies, trend analysis, and elements of TQM. These were all employed with a continuous learning/continuous improvement mindset.

- Fanaticism was absent in applying the management tools. These are tools, not Gods to be worshipped. The managers read widely, understand what is available, and fit the tool to the task. They also know when to discard a tool.
- They are thorough, but not fanatical.
- Each public service agency needs toolmakers.
- Each of us is one of the tools in the tool box. We are responsible for developing ourselves, for staying sharp.

EXPLORATIONS

In our survey we asked: *Some organizations tend to prefer one or two management tools quite universally (TQM, reengineering, etc ...), while other organizations tend to let their choice of management tools depend on a careful analysis of their current problems and needs. How would you describe your organization in this respect?*

Other questions you might ask include:

How long has it been since you inventoried your management tool box? What should be discarded, tuned up, added?

What problems in your organization need new tools?

For each problem, what might be some appropriate tools?

How could you bring the best tools on-stream in a sensible fashion?

How do you stay sharp?

CHAPTER 10

Teamwork

When Carol Beatty, director of the Queen's University School of Industrial Relations, studied 160 teams from the private and public sector to figure out the determinants of success, the team that emerged as the most successful was the RCMP's Project Renewal task force[1] – one of our well-performing organizations.

Few teams could have started in worse times or with a worse mandate. In May 1994 Chief Superintendent Dawson Hovey recommended to the incoming commissioner that the task force be established to deal with the $200 million in budget cuts facing the force. And instead of taking the comparatively easy route of chopping budgets wholesale, Hovey wanted to wield the cuts imaginatively to change the culture and renew the vigor of the organization.

A lot of senior people thought he was nuts – that it was impossible to connect budget cuts to mission and undertake culture change all at the same time. And although he was proposing a team it soon became clear, to his dismay, that he was actually establishing a lightning rod for everyone's anger and frustration. To succeed, he hand-picked a small, talented group of five, including himself and the office manager, some members chosen against the advice of the commissioner but offering Hovey the operational experience he felt would be critical. "Sir," he told the boss, "we need skills, not rank here."

Since five people can't change a 21,000 person police force, they reached out into the various divisions and directorates for allies, who were brought together for a brainstorming session to devise the team's mission statement. "We didn't want us to own anything," he says of the team. "We wanted others to share ownership. We wanted them to buy into the values and the mission."

For the smaller group, the experience was exhilarating. They worked 10- to 12-hour days and on weekends. They held daily bearpit sessions, in which the team came together as a whole to share information and kick around problems. Sometimes several of those sessions would be held during a day. Often the commissioner would pop in to join them. "We'd talk about the dirtiest, snotiest issues. It was like the army. It was very inefficient, yet very effective," says Hovey.

Inefficient, because a lot of time was spent talking and mixing in each other's specialties. Effective, because everybody was sharing and, although people developed specialties, nobody staked out any turf that they then felt compelled to defend. And that included Hovey, who was very careful that as executive director of the team he didn't own the process.

No rank was ever mentioned in the meetings – something that ran against the RCMP culture, which was rank-conscious. Everyone was just a team member, from Hovey to the non-commissioned member of the team (and even to the commissioner, when he dropped in.) And to make that point of equality clear to others, Hovey withdrew from being the sole spokesman to senior management on task force work, as would be the normal practice because of his rank. "At one point, a corporal briefed them. In our organization, that's unheard of. But if you're going to work as a team, your behavior has to be consistent," he says.

Given the long hours and the tough challenge, tensions inevitably arose. "When you have Type-A personalities, you will have friction. But we would deal with it up front. Those issues have to be settled when small or they will become huge problems," he says. For that, the daily meetings were ideal. Issues were easily raised. They could be dealt with openly by everyone, rather than by divisive backroom lobbying and the creation of cliques. In most cases, consensus was reached. Occasionally, when consensus wasn't available, members would agree to disagree but accept the will of the majority and give it their full support.

In the wider force, inevitably, the friction was greater. Project Renewal was cutting 2,300 positions out of a 21,000-person organization. "That can't be done without argument, a lot of resentment, and a lot of emotion," he says. But the allies helped, as did the buy-in from senior levels. And so did the more obviously positive side of task force activity, which included spearheading the grassroots effort to devise a mission, vision, and values statement for the RCMP.

The task force has now wound up. Hovey, in fact, left early, drafted to fill a hole in public relations. But as exciting as his new role is, he still retains a sense of loss for the heightened challenge of Project Renewal and the team camaraderie. "I miss it. I felt devastated when the commissioner asked me to take the other job," he says.

A PARADIGM OF COLLABORATION AND TEAMWORK

As we approach the new millennium, management theorists Warren Bennis and Patricia Biederman say we have to bury the notion of the lone hero and substitute a new paradigm of collaboration and teamwork. "Our mythology refuses to catch up with our reality. We cling to the myth of the Lone Ranger, the romantic idea that great things are usually accomplished by a larger-than-life individual working alone. Despite the evidence to the contrary, we still tend to think of achievement in terms of the Great Man or Great Woman, instead of the Great Group."

They note that in our fascination with solitary genius – from Bill Gates to Steven Spielberg – we tend to underestimate how much creative work is accomplished by groups. And that includes the arts. "A classic example is Michelangelo's masterpiece the ceiling of the Sistine Chapel. In our mind's eye, we see Michelangelo, looking remarkably like Charlton Heston, laboring alone on the scaffolding high above the chapel floor. In fact, thirteen people helped Michelangelo paint the work. Michelangelo was not only an artist, he was, as biographer William E. Wallace points out, the head of a good-sized entrepreneurial enterprise that collaboratively made art that bore his name."[2]

Bennis and Biederman move on to chronicle Great Groups which have altered society's shared reality in some way, like the Manhattan Project and the Disney animators. Most of us will never belong to a Great Group. But we often belong to groups. We are routinely members of teams, committees, and task forces, where teamwork is essential, and though we may not alter society's shared reality we can certainly change the shared reality of our organization and its stakeholders.

Increasingly, organizations are turning to teamwork and teams. Canada's magazine for entrepreneurs, *Profit*, in its 1997 celebration of growth, found that many of the country's fastest-growing companies started as team efforts. And they continue to grow through sharing and teamwork. "As business becomes more and more complex, entrepreneurs are giving up the 'lone wolf' shtick for the power of teamwork," *Profit* noted. The four Serruya brothers, who run Yogen Früz, the world's largest franchiser of frozen yogurt with more than 3,000 stores in 74 countries, meet every weeknight, from 7 to 9 p.m., to talk shop. If one's traveling, they link by conference call.[3] Like the RCMP, they've learned the power of sharing every day, realizing the investment in time pays off.

Our well-performing organizations expressed support for teamwork through their mission and value statements, their leadership style, and their daily actions. They used teams for a variety of tasks – from developing strategic plans to delivering services and replacing the old hierarchical structures. While the variation in teams was considerable – more so than any of the other eight factors – and evolving, every one of the agencies displayed a clear and ever-present sense of teamwork. They were consistently collegial and considerate, inside and outside of teams.

Managers were expected to be team players – even when their organization made limited use of actual teams. Our respondents felt that a team-player attitude was critical when interacting with peers and others outside the agency. That included, as we've shown, trying to embrace outside stakeholders as partners rather than excluding them as opponents. In today's more complicated and complex world, one person rarely has all the answers.

TEAMWORK PATTERNS

Of course, like so many management innovations, teams aren't new. For most of us, the fondest memories of work have come through teamwork, be it in a specialized task force, a management committee, or a two-person informal partnership carrying out similar or complementary tasks. The classic manager-secretarial relationship is a team – generally a strong and enduring one. While the use of teams is certainly growing, and the power devolved to them increasing, the trend is definitely not a fad. A fad will vanish, like the hula hoop. Teams won't fade because, as public-service organizations edge out of silos and work horizontally, teams are essential for gathering multi-disciplinary people together.

In the past, staff in an organization used to work side-by-side with individuals of the same discipline, but each individual would effectively toil alone. Today the nature of work requires more sharing and, hence, more teams and teamwork. And many people prefer to work in teams, for their personal satisfaction. Recognizing that, and caring about their people, managers are now creating more team opportunities.

Two organizations in our survey had developed teams and teamwork in ways that literally turned traditional pyramidal organizational structure upside down. We've already looked at Muskogee Veterans Benefits' introduction of self-managed work teams to dramatically improve processing productivity. The Australian Public Service Commission used a team approach to design and then adopt a new organization also built entirely on self-managed work teams. As a result, the agency's organizational diagram is shaped more like an inverted pyramid, with the chief executive, other managers and the change facilitation team supporting the self-managed work groups. The self-directed teams are responsible for all work in a geographical slice of the country or in a specialized area like personnel.

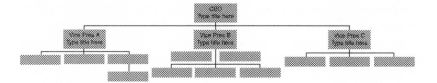

Traditional organization chart

The shift to work teams appears more pronounced for those agencies in our sample that were established in the past decade. Unencumbered by tradition, hierarchy, and vested interests, they moved to new forms more easily. At the same time, and despite their long histories, some longer-established organizations have moved just as boldly, dismantling the old organization rather than grafting teams onto it.

Among our respondents, the scope of teams progressed in steps from a loose, fairly unstructured level of ad-hoc or part-time teams and committees mandated only to develop recommendations, to formal, long-lived, permanent, and self-directed teams with real and extensive decision-making authority. At the first level, an orga-

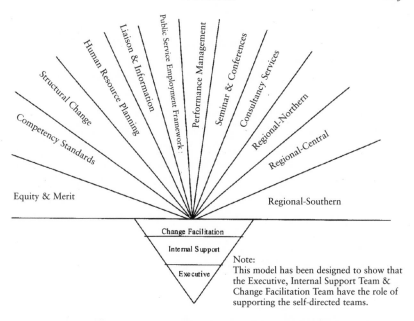

Australian Public Service Optional Organization Chart

nization might simply declare teamwork a fundamental, underlying value, while only using work teams in limited fashion. At the second step, work teams are common, along with the committees. At the top step, self-directed teams are a driving force for the organization.

We found well-performing organizations at all stages of that continuum. It seems those at the final stage had progressed through the earlier steps. Significantly, all of our surveyed organizations reported that they intend in future to amplify the use of teams, either by expanding them at the current level of operation or by advancing to the next stage.

Illustrating the different levels, we could start with New Brunswick Human Resources Development, which had no overall strategy or framework for high performing teams. Teams handle some ministry work and are growing in importance, but no consistent approach exists.

The Singapore Central Provident Fund Board works as a team, or, as they put it, a family: "If front-line staff have difficulty serving a customer, colleagues, supervisors, managers, and top management are expected to help. ... Staff are encouraged to help answer a phone call while their colleague is busy serving a customer, or to help clear paperwork after office hours if a particular section is overloaded with work." On top of this underlying valuing of teamwork, each employee is a member of several work teams (the agency has 90 for work improvement alone), and management is constantly on the lookout for impediments and disruptions to teamwork.

The New Zealand Ministry of Foreign Affairs and Trade has no planning department. Instead, each year a newly composed team develops and shepherds the ministry's strategic plan. The team includes representatives from across the organization, including junior and senior staff, managers and line staff, and different occupational groups. For each year's effort, a different member of the senior management team assumes the chair. The ministry uses similar teams to set up new embassies and for other planning tasks. Occasionally they establish two teams with slightly different terms of reference to see what innovative thinking might result.

Other agencies employ teams more systematically. Statistics Canada, for example, launches all team projects of any significance with a review and approval of the team's objectives, broad methodology, and total cost. Other teams design and deliver staff training. Teams of middle managers tackle a current problem affecting the wider organization and propose solutions.

Self-directed work teams have a full-time membership that is responsible for a specific product or service to an internal or external client. At Muskogee Veterans Benefits, the various teams cover fields from compensation to education to loan guaranty, with many taking on colorful monikers such as Edu-Gators, Loan Sharks, The Service Station, and Trekkors.

Our survey found that teams also respond to crises. That is a bit at odds with the standard philosophy that in a crisis one reverts to the traditional military model of command and control, with information flowing up and directions flowing down from a single source at the top. Yet at the United States Defense Mapping Agency, work teams headed by lower-level employees provided support for military actions such as the Gulf War. The teams operate free of bureaucratic constraints, coping with the high stress, urgent deadlines, and the critical service needs of a crisis situation. When New Zealand faced the prospect of renewed nuclear testing by France in the South Pacific, the ministry responded by setting up a team to study the situation.

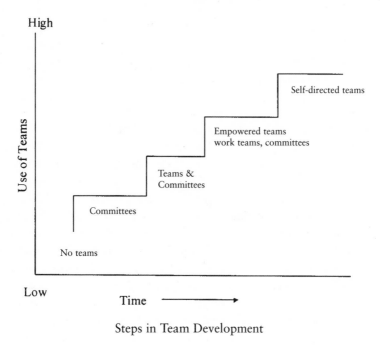

Steps in Team Development

BEATTY ON SUCCESSFUL TEAMS

Project Renewal was also a response to a crisis. That challenge may have contributed to its top ranking in the Beatty study, since the groups she studied had to fill out a performance self-assessment and the RCMP group was highly enthusiastic, with a propensity to give itself the highest marks. But as we've pointed out before, the RCMP isn't prone to exaggerate its successes. And Project Renewal's strengths conform neatly to Beatty's model for successful teams.

She discovered that 88 per cent of the performance variance in her 160 teams could be predicted by just two variables: problem-solving skills and conflict-handling skills. Her conclusion that problem-solving skills are important sounds obvious, almost tautological, since that's what so many teams are set up to do. But solving problems in a team is not an obvious matter. We've all seen groups where ten people, each with an IQ of over 125, lock themselves in a room, work day and night, and then emerge with a feeble report that looks like it was prepared by one person with too little sleep. A team should be greater than the sum of its parts. But often managers have no idea how to make a team more intelligent than the individual members.

Team members must bring a range of talents to the table. They must communicate effectively with one another. They must build on one another's ideas, so that the final result is better than any one person's notions. Beatty's research shows that such synergy will occur if the team establishes a team mission at the start, to help sessions run more smoothly, and if they occasionally evaluate the team against those standards. Team members must accept an equal commitment and shared responsibility for the activities of the group. They should strive for consensus but not group-think.

The team must be capable of confronting disrupters and dealing with conflicts. Often teams can't handle conflict, Beatty says, because the rules weren't established at the start. "When conflict arises, they have no process to handle it. It's hard enough to handle conflict ordinarily," she notes. "It's even more difficult in teams."

Too often teams are thrown together with no training and no mission statement. Then the team is told the normal rules are suspended. That can be exciting. But it also can hand too much leeway to team members and lead to conflict. Sometimes that conflict won't be readily apparent because some members withdraw rather than bring their concerns to the fore. Nevertheless, the conflict will be steadily taking its toll on the team. "The good teams will draw out the people who don't talk. A good team will also take on the people who talk too much," advises Beatty.

In an effective team, people will pitch in if someone is sick, Beatty says. But they don't let chronic shirkers escape from completing work. They also don't tolerate cliques and sub-groups, which can pose a great danger. "You get in-groups and out-groups. The out-groups won't contribute," says Beatty.

One of our problems in developing a team culture is that we lack proper models. Sports tends to be the main analogy and while that can be appropriate for ad hoc teams, with clear goals and a definite timeline, Beatty contends it's deeply misleading for the ongoing work group. A better model, she stresses, is the family – a lesson that comes naturally to the teams in our sample from Singapore, Egypt, and the Phillipines but has to be learned by those in the more competitive North American culture.

"In sports, you play the game and go home. But in a work team, where your livelihood is on the line and relationships are long term, it's like a family," Beatty explains. "We expect work teams to operate like sports teams. But the work is so much vaguer. The sports team develops skills, practises, plays the game, and analyses the results. With work teams, the results aren't always immediate, the innovations are always occurring – new technology coming on stream. It's like a sports team where the rules or game keep changing. You couldn't practise or might practise the wrong thing. You practise throwing a football and it's basketball today."

SIZE AND SKILLS

Beatty's study found that team size plays a role in determining both problem-solving and conflict-handling skills. Her research showed that 5 to 7 members appeared best. Once the size exceeds 12, effectiveness is not high.

Team Conflict-Handling Skills

Queen's University professor Carol Beatty sets the following guidelines for effectively handling conflicts in teams:

- don't avoid important issues and hope they will go away;
- adopt a win-win orientation to solving conflict with other group members;
- don't allow aggressive individuals to take over;
- don't be afraid of confronting emotional individuals;
- confront issues in a sensitive, non-judgmental way;
- assume goodwill and good intentions on the part of your team members;
- don't allow group members to breach the group norms.

But Jon Katzenbach and Douglas K. Smith, from the U.S. consulting firm McKinsey and Company, studied more than 50 teams in 30 companies and organizations, from Motorola to Operation Desert Storm and the Girl Scouts. They found that effective teams can range from two people to 25. In their book *The Wisdom of Teams: Creating the High-Performance Organization*, they argue that small size is more of a pragmatic guide than an absolute necessity for success.[4]

They found that diversity was needed in three categories of skills: technical or functional expertise, problem-solving and decision-making skills, and interpersonal skills. "In all the successful teams we encountered, not one had all the needed skills at the outset. ... In fact, we discovered that teams are powerful vehicles for developing the skills needed to meet the team's performance challenge. Accordingly, team member selection ought to ride as much on skill potential as on skills already proven," they note.

They stress that no group ever becomes a team unless it can hold itself accountable as a team. "At its core, team accountability is about the sincere promises we make to ourselves and others, promises that underpin two critical aspects of effective teams: commitment and trust," they write.

Peter Senge, in *The Fifth Discipline*, stresses the importance of mastering the practices of dialogue and discussion for effective teams. Group members must learn what he calls a "deep listening" to one another on complex issues and must be able to suspend their own views. "Lastly, the discipline of team learning, like any discipline, requires practice. Yet, this is exactly what teams in modern organizations lack. Imagine trying to build a great theatre ensemble or a great symphony orchestra without rehearsal. Imagine a championship sports team without practice. In fact, the process whereby such teams learn is through continual movement between practice and performance, practice, performance, practice again, perform again," he says.[5]

Top managers form a special team that generally serves as the key forum for strategic dialogue in the organization. The nine factors in our book are interwoven into their work, both as topics for conversation and as elements for making their team thrive. Siobhan Alderson, of University of Leeds, in *Personnel Review* set out six key competence areas for top management teams that echo our own findings:[6]

- interpersonal relationships must be good and team members must understand one another's values and management styles;
- there must be a capacity for openness so any issues that require discussion can be discussed;
- the members must have a high degree of trust in each other;

- the team must be approachable, accepting feedback and criticism with maturity;
- the team must have sufficient discipline and cohesion to implement the decisions on which they agree;
- the team must have the capacity to discuss and understand both long- and short-term issues.

BUILDING SUCCESSFUL TEAMS

Organizations seeking more effective use of teams should begin by asking basic questions about the agency. Is the work better done in teams or by individuals? Do the mission and values support teamwork? Do the leadership and accountability systems foster its development? Are employees supportive of teamwork? Do they have the skills and attitudes to work in teams? What has been the organization's previous experience with teams – is it something to build on, to learn from, or to avoid? What model of teamwork would best suit the situation: simple, empowered, or self-directed? What roadblocks exist and how can they be removed?

The second step is to ensure that a number of prerequisites for teams are in place. An infrastructure needs to be created to pull teams, rather than trail their development. Our survey found that the further an organization was along the work-team path, the more likely it was that such an infrastructure was in place. Even then, this support was initially an afterthought rather than a strategically planned effort to move the organization to greater teamwork.

Revenue Canada has the right approach: teamwork is a principle outlined in their strategic planning documents. Selection, competitions, performance appraisals, awards, and in-house training in teamwork all reinforce that principle. They ensure each team has a clear mandate, decision-making authority, the ability to design operations, and shared responsibility for results.

Organizations should consider embedding teamwork in their mission. The National Library of Canada's mission statement outlines the general principles under which teams are expected to operate. Attention is paid to defining objectives, setting terms of reference, selecting members, and establishing reporting and communication lines. The library's values, explicitly stated in the mission, are also conducive to effective teamwork.

Agencies should give training in teamwork, conflict resolution,

and win-win styles. The United States Defense Mapping Agency
recognizes that teamwork is not natural for everyone and prepares
for crises through extensive training in teamwork, by providing
feedback on work teams, and by including that feedback in performance appraisals.

At the Singapore Defense Ministry, officers are trained in teamwork and all staff attend six half-day workshops held to promote
an understanding of teamwork and team building concepts. An
experiential two-day session follows in which they apply the newly
learned skills.

Muskogee Veterans Benefits gives extensive training to teams.
The topics include defining the role of a coach, team leader and
team member; the difference between traditional management and
a team-based organization; the stages of group development; the
dysfunctional behaviors of teams in transition; how to hold effective meetings; problem-solving techniques for teams; the tools of
brainstorming, multi-voting and consensus; communication and listening skills; and dealing with difficult people. All those topics,
obviously, are important to teams and if members are not attuned
to them, they are more likely to stumble.

Investing In Employee-Managed Teams

The Department of Veterans Affairs regional benefit office in
Muskogee, Oklahoma, has developed a one-page sheet of advice
for those organizations that wish to invest in employee-managed
teams. Some excerpts:

Commitment
- Obtain executive commitment to employee-managed teams.
- Commit a large share of resources to the transformation of your
  organization to a team-based environment, including physical
  and emotional support.
- Be willing to listen and work with your employees.
- Emphasize the importance of leadership in a team-based environ-
  ment.

Goals
- Keep all employees apprised on organizational goals.
- Allow teams to establish their own goals that coincide with orga-
  nizational goals.

Parameters
- Define the new roles of employees in your team organization and ensure they understand their roles.
- Determine who has decision-making responsibility.

Training
- Train your management staff first. Managers must mentally redefine their position from that of supervisor to leader.
- Train employees in problem-solving and decision-making skills, how to improve interaction and communication with each other, and how to incorporate continuous improvement into their work processes.

Empowerment
- Management must encourage and allow teams to make decisions on thier own.
- Initially shift decisions that are less complex and difficult to teams. As teams become more mature, they will be capable of more difficult decisions, with more serious consequences.
- Provide as much data as possible to the teams.
- Give ownership of your process or service to "nearest-point" decision makers.

Recognition
- Reward team performance rather than individual performance.
- Management should reward a team when they begin making accomplishments and achieving or exceeding their goals.
- Remember to recognize small wins.

Those examples show that teamwork is not natural. It requires training. That team training should involve practice, working together in simulations, or tackling real management problems in a training setting.

Attention must also be given to recruiting and selecting team players. As those who studied teams have shown, this can be a tricky task. Managers of our well-performing organizations tend to select a diverse group of people for teams, preferring individuals they know are able to work in a team. The National Library of Canada notes that although membership on some committees is still generally linked to one's position in the organization and responsibility for overseeing a certain activity, management is placing an increasing emphasis "on the expertise and skills that each member brings to the group as distinct from the authority embodied in the position he or she occupies."

The Singapore Defense Ministry selects for each work team based on the specific criteria for the task. One useful model for team selection and team process is Edward de Bono's Six Hats.[7] Getting people on the team with particular strength in each of those conceptual competencies, as well as all the technical competencies, is important, as is valuing those who wear a hat different from yours, even though they may be a little tedious when they keep waving it.

Organizations must also design management and accountability systems that support teamwork. The intangible reward of personal satisfaction from working on a Great Group is wonderful, but the tangible rewards, pay and recognition, are also important. As we've mentioned, New Brunswick Human Resources Development has been struggling with just that issue, as it tries to bring in its pay-for-performance scheme.

Lastly, it's important to stress that teams are comprised of individuals. They will tend to have leaders. Bennis and Biederman found that every Great Group had a strong leader. "This is one of the paradoxes of creative collaboration. Great groups are made up of people with rare gifts working together as equals. Yet, in virtually every one there is one person who acts as maestro, organizing the genius of others. He or she is a pragmatic dreamer, a person with an original but attainable vision. Ironically, the leader is able to realize his or her dream only if the others are free to do exceptional work," they observe.

Many of the Great Groups they studied were start-ups, which are more likely to have one individual initially breathing life into the idea. It's unclear whether that model holds for groups in an existing workplace. In some of our well-performing organizations, teams had clear leaders. In others, rotation seemed preferred. Muskogee Veterans Benefits views all employees as empowered leaders within a concept "which strives to demonstrate teamwork analogous to that of geese flying in formation. Observers have concluded that as each bird flaps its wings, it creates an uplift for the bird immediately following. When the leading goose gets tired, it rotates back in the formation and another flies at the point. By flying in this manner, the flock may double the flying range of any individual."

As with all management tools, teams aren't magical solutions to organizational problems. But teams, and teamwork, are an increasing aspect of organizational life today. They can be effective in short-term situations, leading change, as with the RCMP's Project Renewal. They can be productive in carrying out the day-to-day work of organizations, as Muskogee Veterans Benefits shows. The era of the Lone Ranger is over. Teamwork is a watchword of the 1990s and will be a guiding principal in the future.*

CAPSULES

- Some of the reasons for Project Renewal's success: ownership was shared, issues were extensively discussed by all, rank was eschewed, and tensions were dealt with openly at an early stage. Also, with only five members, the team was small.
- Management theorist Warren Bennis says we have to bury the notion of the lone hero and substitute a new paradigm of collaboration and teamwork.
- Remember that the Sistine Chapel was painted by a 14-person team rather than just a solo effort by Michelangelo.
- While the variation in teams in our well-performing sample was considerable, and evolving, every one of the agencies displayed a clear and ever-present sense of teamwork. They were consistently collegial and considerate, inside and outside teams.
- The trend to teams won't soon vanish, like the hula hoop, because as public-service organizations edge out of silos and work horizontally, teams are essential for bringing multi-disciplinary people together.
- Among our respondents, the scope of teams progressed in steps from a loose, fairly unstructured level of ad-hoc or part-time teams and committees mandated only to develop recommenda-

---

* There were infrequent references to teamwork with the public service unions. Admittedly, we did not ask directly about this topic. From personal experience, it is an important issue. It can be improved through using some of the skills noted in the chapters on people and on teamwork in discussing the management-union relationship. For example, taking negotiation and problem-solving skills courses together to facilitate dialogue.

tions to formal, long-lived, permanent, and self-directed teams with real and extensive decision-making authority.

- Carol Beatty discovered that 88 per cent of the performance variance in her 160 teams could be predicted by just two variables: problem-solving skills and conflict handling skills.
- She found it helpful for the team to establish a team mission at the start and to occasionally evaluate the team against those standards. Team members must establish an equal commitment and shared responsibility for the activities of the group. They should strive for consensus but not group-think.
- She also found that the team must be capable of confronting disrupters and dealing with conflicts.
- The family, rather than sports teams, should be our model for work teams.
- Research seems divided on whether large teams can be effective. Clearly, small teams can be.
- The team must find the right mix of skills in three categories: technical or functional expertise, problem-solving and decision-making skills, and interpersonal skills.
- Katzenbach and Smith stress that no group ever becomes a team unless it can hold itself accountable as a team.
- Organizations seeking more effective use of teams should begin by asking basic questions about the agency.
- An infrastructure needs to be created to pull teams, rather than trail their development.
- Organizations should consider embedding teamwork in the mission.
- Agencies should give training in teamwork, conflict resolution, and win-win styles.
- Attention must also be given to recruiting and selecting team players.
- Remember that teams will have leaders. Sometimes Great Leaders. Sometimes rotational leaders, like geese flying in formation.
- Teamwork is a watchword of the 1990s and will be a guiding principle in the future.

EXPLORATIONS

In our survey we asked: *What can you say about the way your organization relates to teams and teamwork (selection; training; for*

*what purposes; permanent teams versus ad hoc teams; deadlines;
accountability; rewards ...)?*

Other useful questions might include:

Which work in your agency is better done in teams
or by individuals?

What has been the organization's previous experience with teams – is it something to build on, to
learn from, or to avoid?

What model of teamwork would best suit the situation: simple, empowered, or self-directed?

What changes are required to conform to that
model?

Do the mission and values support teamwork?

Do the leadership and accountability systems support the development of teamwork?

Are employees supportive of teamwork?

What skills are needed for the people on various
teams?

What roadblocks to teams exist and how can they
be removed?

CHAPTER 11

Change Management

They were called Change Champions. The squad, elected by their colleagues from the various departments in the New Brunswick Human Resources Development, traveled to head office monthly for a wide-ranging look at management's restructuring efforts. They offered advice and then returned to their units to report directly to fellow staff about the latest elements of the ministry's change initiatives.

To encourage frankness, line managers weren't invited to Change Champion conclaves. That meant the front-line workers serving as Change Champions would return to their workplace better informed than their bosses about the latest ministry plans. In a world where information is power, managers had been superseded on a crucial front by underlings. "That made it bumpy at first," acknowledges deputy-minister Karen Mann. "We then began to send the agenda out to managers. I think that made them more comfortable."

The Change Champions were just one novel aspect of her ministry's change management strategy. The effort was triggered in 1992 by a $60 million overrun on the $340 million budget, as welfare cases soared in the recession. The budget has now been trimmed back to $289 million, 27 per cent less than was spent in 1992, and staff has been chopped by about the same percentage, from 550 to 395 employees. Despite that cutback, cases are handled more quickly and more intelligently today, as the ministry machinery has been reconfigured to promote client self-sufficiency rather than simply keep handing out money to people trapped in the grips of welfare dependency.

After the brainstorming that led to the ministry's provocative three-word mission statement – create client self-sufficiency – teams were established to take a similarly unconventional look at their work processes. Each committee was asked, "If you could rewrite the books, how would the ministry look?"

Behind that wide-open invitation was the belief that in public service organizations staff live in fear of the auditor-general. When slapped on the fingers by the auditor for some flaw, be it minor or major, a department tends to quadruple its efforts to come up with sure-fire methods to ensure that such public censure will never happen again. Ten years later, nobody knows the reasons for the cumbersome work procedures – but nobody is willing to change them either. This ministry, however, decided to delve back to first principles.

An initial suggestion was to eliminate the second signature on forms. With a second signature, the team argued, nobody was actually taking full responsibility and work was being needlessly duplicated. The front-line worker was signing and kicking the matter upstairs, comfortable that ultimate responsibility now lay elsewhere. But the boss, desk overloaded with paper, was often signing unthinkingly, trusting the subordinate to have screened sufficiently. The buzzword of the time was empowerment. The department realized it had to delegate, in a serious way, to the front-line worker – and make him or her accountable, rather than continue the charade of accountability bound up in the second signature.

QUICK HITS AND OTHER CHANGES

The ministry was intent on scoring some quick hits that would provide reassurance to staff that the change process was actually working. Second signature was appealing as a quick hit, because it was dramatic. But, as it turned out, it was too dramatic for the central agencies and political masters. In the end, it took two years to hit the bullseye.

In the interval, technology provided some quick hits. The ministry hired Andersen Consulting Inc. to assist. The consultants recommended the Change Champions process and spearheading an initiative to reduce paperwork through modern technology. That initiative quickly produced results – and those results continued for several years, turning a mountain into a molehill. "For every 8 inches of paper, we took it down to half an inch of paper," says Mann.

In the past, citizens seeking welfare would have to visit a Human Resources Development office and wait to meet a case officer, who would fill out forms by hand during a 45-minute interview. The client would be sent away and told to return again for a second interview in a few weeks, after welfare eligibility had been determined. In the revamped system, people call in and explain their situation in a ten-minute chat with a worker who uses computerized templates to determine instantaneously whether the person is eligible. A cheque can then be produced overnight. A meeting with a counselor is immediately scheduled for the client so that they can quickly begin the more important part of the process: reviewing the economic, social, and educational factors that led the individual to welfare and building a plan for attaining self-sufficiency. "We want to deal with the whole person. First we deal with the financial crisis and then we get onto the real issues," says Mann. "Before we didn't deal with anything other than the financial requirements."

Originally, the ministry had calculated its employees spent 70 per cent of their time on administration and 30 per cent on client contact. The goal was to flip that so 70 per cent of staff time would be spent with clients. That objective has yet to be met, but is within reach.

The agency also decided to institute performance indicators. But it was aware that could backfire by threatening employees. During change, says Mann, "you have to create trust that there will be no reprisals. It takes time for people to believe you." Having forged that trust, top officials were careful not to squander it. Staff was therefore promised that management would not evaluate individual performance for two years after the new measures were in place, so employees wouldn't be blamed if the measures were inappropriate or if the change process itself was hampering them from achieving targets. "People won't perform at their best when uncertain," says Mann.

The downsizing, of course, was a giant obstacle to trust. Managers planned, re-planned, and again re-planned every element, trying to minimize the hurt to individuals. Once specific downsizing numbers were released to front-line employees, managers had to balance just and equitable treatment for employees with a need to complete essential tasks such as identifying which employees would remain with the organization.

That's the nature of change: lots of things happen simultaneously and you can't isolate them. You have to perform well on all fronts. Ministry staff had to manage current service delivery, design the future service delivery model and processes, incorporate new technology into the workplace, and adjust to significant personnel changes from job loss and job restructuring. That combined to create a stressful work environment that was simultaneously exciting and threatening – and certainly full of tension.

All of the department's job descriptions were rewritten to conform to the re-engineered workplace. Staff who wanted to opt out could take advantage of a voluntary separation program. Others were interviewed by managers and asked their first and second preference for positions in the revamped workplace. It was a modified job interview: everyone had completed a self-assessment and the meeting focused on how their talents fit the posts they were seeking.

Managers then gathered in what Mann remembers as gut-wrenching sessions, deciding who got the positions they wanted and who would be bumped out. They picked the Tuesday after a long weekend to inform staff, believing that would allow support to be given at the workplace for the remainder of the week to those who needed it. On D-Day, everything was tightly choreographed. Each employee had an appointed time to meet with management and learn his or her fate. The staff quickly divided into what Mann calls the mads, the sads, and the glads. "I'll never forget that day as long as I live," she says.

In time, those who remained were energized. Where possible, those terminated have been redeployed elsewhere in the government. "People are feeling secure now. Before, there was thought to be an invisible life-long contract in the public service – working for less than ideal wages in return for security. When that was broken, everyone was shocked. Now people are a lot more realistic. They realize all organizations – including government – must change. People will work hard but they also feel that they don't owe you anything," Mann says.

UNDERSTANDING THE CONTOURS OF CHANGE

What stands out about that story is how common it is today. All public service organizations are undergoing change today and the story of Karen Mann and New Brunswick Human Resources

Development simply reminds us of our own workplace. "Change is a perpetual process which does not stop so long as we seek better results," Lebanon's Civil Service Board observes.

To some extent, that state of affairs really isn't new: Disraeli in 1867, facing the breakup of the British Empire and the burgeoning industrial revolution, noted that "change is inevitable. In a progressive country, change is constant." But clearly the pace of change and its scope has heightened today, in society and, notably, in public sector organizations. Two decades ago, government bureaucracies were structured so that buffers prevented change. Managers didn't have to be change agents. Indeed, they were supposed to limit the damage from change. Today, for our well-performing organizations, managing change is a requisite skill of modern public-service administration.

The word change is used so frequently today that we tend to lump all change together. But it's important for managers to study the contours of change, because it appears in different forms and with different force and frequency. While managers have to accept that change is an unstoppable impetus, they also must understand the specific nature of the change occurring in their workplace today and the change heading there tomorrow, so they can manage it.

Our study unearthed three useful ways of categorizing change. The first is by size. Some change is massive, hitting the organization after a wide-ranging reassessment. On other occasions, change is incremental, the continuous improvement and continuous adjustment of an organization navigating towards its North Star or Southern Cross.

Change can also be characterized by the degree to which it is externally or internally propelled. In the same way that geologists want to know the chemical composition of the material they mine, managers will find it helpful to determine the internal-external composition of the change they are digging through. It falls into three categories:

1   Primarily internal change, driven by continuous improvement or strategic initiatives in an effort to improve service and reduce cost. Obviously such change will be in harmony with the changing external environment, but its impetus and driving force is internal, the mission. In that sense, it's discretionary.

2   Externally driven change. Such change flows from the evolving

demands of government and the public. It's a combination of non-discretionary and discretionary change: some transformation is required but the specific actions might be quite discretionary. As far as possible, well-performing organizations think these matters out in advance and take measures to prepare for change rather than simply reacting with more limited options at the last moment. Many agencies in our sample, for example, had been or were being downsized – cuts of 10 to 50 per cent were common over the past decade and more were expected. This is change which the organization can strategically determine how to respond to.

3 Finally, some change is environmental, driven externally by the effects of factors such as technology and globalization. Again, such change is at the same time both non-discretionary and discretionary. Our organizations try to predict, understand, and make use of these changes – to lead, not trail.

The third way of looking at change was offered by Canada's National Library, and could best be described as Good Change or Bad Change. Good Change is in harmony with the mandate and allows the organization to achieve its goals better. It should be embraced and nourished. Bad Change is at cross-purposes with the mandate. It needs to be managed and minimized. Managers can influence, but not fully control staff reaction to change. But it's easier to gain employee acceptance for Good Change – change that clearly will improve the organization.

"Accepting new technology was never a problem at the Library," says Chief Librarian Marianne Scott, "as the staff saw it as an improvement. They wanted to gobble up new technology as it allows them to do their work better. It's when the service is eroding that change is very difficult." Echoing many downsized workplaces, she adds that staff felt "they were doing things very well but managers are now saying we may have to do things less superbly well. That's hard for people to accept."

MISSION AND PEOPLE, AGAIN

In managing change, all the other attributes of public service management we have been exploring in this book play a vital role. The organization must have leadership to guide the way; trust and communication to keep everybody together; and teamwork, appropriate management tools, and accountability during and after the process. But two attributes exceed all the others in importance: mission and people. The organization must have a firm sense of its goals or it won't be able to distinguish between mere change and improvement. The organization must also be skilled in handling its people through a time of personal and organizational turmoil, if not trauma.

Barbara Moses, author of *Career Intelligence*,[1] frowns on the many managers today who breathlessly rattle on and on about the changing workplace, not understanding the terror that strikes in their employees. What might be a talisman of success for managers may be a harbinger of doom for their staff. Our well-performing organizations are aware of that danger, however, because they are preoccupied with the people-side of change. Indeed they stressed it much more than we've seen in any text on change management.

"Change is always feared by people and in this case our employees are no exception," advised Egypt's Cabinet Information Unit. Singapore's Ministry of Defense echoed, "There is no doubt change creates feelings of initial resistance, insecurity, uncertainty, loss, and fear in our people." And in Denmark, the industrial injuries board added: "It is perfectly natural that a thorough restructuring process causes frustration in the whole organization. It is understandable that it is hard for some people to accept that the tasks they have been performing for maybe 25 years have now disappeared. Irrespective of the amount of energy put into this work, we do not get out of the restructuring without getting hurt. But our goal is to limit this as much as possible."

Saskatchewan Highways and Transportation pointed out that the bulk of employees hit by organizational change experience the grief cycle made famous by Elisabeth Kubler-Ross in her work on death and dying. They move from status quo to stunned paralysis, to denial, to anger, to bargaining, to depression, to testing, and finally to acceptance. "The rate at which individuals pass though this grief cycle appears to be determined by individual traits, beliefs, perceptions of their work environment, and wholeness of their personal lives," writes Deputy Minister Clare Kirkland. "Individuals exposed to significant changes as a group have stated feelings of safety when part of the group and feelings of insecurity when away from the group. Others isolate or retreat to where they feel comfortable."

Specifically, the losses that arise are:

- loss of attachments to specific relationships or groups;
- loss of turf, from physical territory to fields of responsibility;
- loss of structure, such as patterns of authority, policies, schedules, deadlines and physical arrangements;
- loss of future, be it perceived or real;
- loss of meaning, expressed in the oft-heard phrase, "I just can't understand why they ...";
- loss of control, as everything seems up for grabs.

Some employees express their anger, but most internalize it. "If anything can aid in the process from a productivity perspective it is to get people to anger quickly and through it in a safe environment. Overall productivity in those not involved in planning the change is noticeably lower during and immediately after the change," Kirkland observes.

To help cope with change, many of our respondents provide training in the nature of change and how to reduce its impact on staff. Revenue Canada's workshops dwell on the grief process and coping mechanisms. Employees develop a personal planner, listing what actions they can take for themselves during change and what the organization might contribute. The subtext: it's permissible to have personal concerns – and negative feelings – during change.

Even good change, seen to be advancing the mission, can be traumatic and have its downside for staff. The sixteenth century British theologian Richard Hooker summed it up: "Change is not made without inconvenience, even from worse to better."[3]

This preoccupation by our well-performing agencies with change's impact is consistent with their high valuation of people. It is also, we suspect, a key distinguishing feature between agencies which handle change successfully and those that don't, a fact which is not mentioned enough.

THE CONSERVATISM OF NATURE

In understanding the contours of change, it's also important to wipe away the image and impulse we all have about Big Bang change – of managers being able to figure out what is needed, create a new universe in one explosive moment of redefinition, and get it all right. Major change doesn't happen that way, and imagining it does can derail or destroy the process.

Generally, in a strategic planning effort an organization starts with a level of performance that's quite low. After all, why bother seeking major change if performance isn't significantly below expectations? The management usually meets, preferably in a rustic retreat, and comes to a new understanding of how the organization should perform. The mood of those managers is now ecstatic. Their perception of performance has shot up, although performance itself hasn't changed one iota since they've been locked in a stuffy room far from the workplace.

When they return to their offices, they look as if they're on drugs. They're dazed, giddy – and high. With the leaders detached from reality, staff inevitably diverts its attention to them, wondering what will happen next. As employees hear management prating on about how "people are our most important resource," or similar retreat-induced nostrums, the staff start to worry and doubt. Performance generally dips, to below the lousy performance of before – and well below the exalted level that the managers magically expected to occur on the Big Bang day of their return from the retreat. So the end result of the strategic planning exercise, a few weeks into the transformation, is almost always lower performance.

And that essentially continues, in our experience, for six to eight months. Performance remains flat, or at best only minimally higher than at the outset. Ole, who has suffered through this several times, notes from bitter experience that at this juncture the manager who initiated strategic planning finds his or her best friends coming in to talk cautiously about his or her formerly spectacular career. "One major mistake out of so many successes won't make a difference," they say soothingly, as they point to staff resistance. "Your reputation won't be tarnished. But it's time to face the music. It was good to discuss these things and healthy for the organization but we live in the real world and it has not done the trick. Let's try something else or go back to the way we were before."

That is a defining moment in organizational life when leaders, in front of their team, have to stand confidently behind their work. They must become a one-person critical mass, warning: "I'm not backing down. If you don't wish to follow, a conflict will occur between us." In particular, they must not sanction the tempting term everybody is repeating: staff resistance. That just abdicates

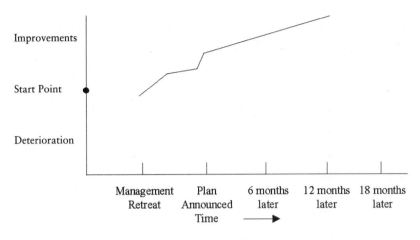

Strategic planning – the text book

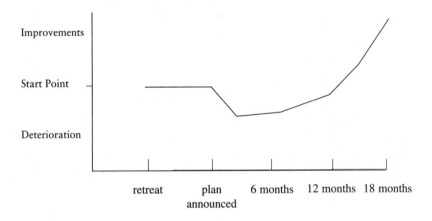

Strategic planning – the reality

management's responsibility for change by suggesting it's the scum down below causing the problem. It's also highly unproductive to label as resistors the very people you depend on to provide superior performance.

If the leader persists, experience shows that somehow performance will gradually start to improve. The organization edges into a learning mode where it better understands the forces affecting it and is better disposed to capitalize on events. The agency starts to believe the leader is serious because he or she *is* serious. And the organization starts to perform better.

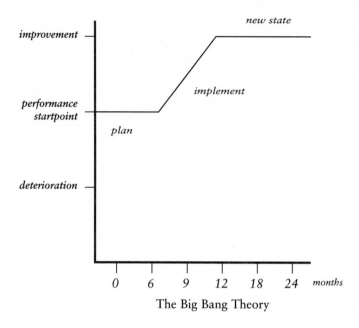

The Big Bang Theory

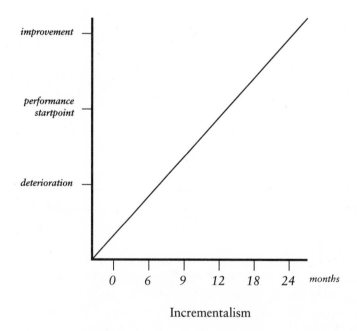

Incrementalism

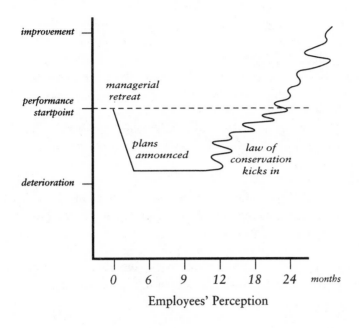

Employees' Perception

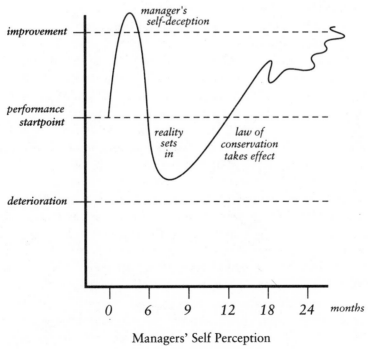

Managers' Self Perception

Different Views of Change

This stutter-step transformation can best be explained by the conservatism of nature principle expressed by the French chemist and metallurgist Henri Louis Le Chatelier. Imagine attaching a thin string to a rowboat and trying to pull it. Initially the rowboat stays firmly in place, refusing to budge. Suddenly, without you increasing your force, the boat starts to move. When you stop pulling, the rowboat will continue unabated for awhile before coming to a halt. In both starting and stopping the rowboat, the conservatism of nature must be overcome.

Human beings are part of nature. It's inevitable that the same conservatism will be encountered in trying to pull them along. It's therefore important that managers expect and plan for a delay in reaction when they start applying the technologies or other innovations of a transformation effort. That knowledge won't necessarily make the period a less dangerous or nerve-wracking experience: even when you understand what's happening, it's tortuous. But if you understand that the lag is an intrinsic principle of nature, you are more likely to carry the process through to the end and maintain a solid relationship with employees.

Waiting can be difficult for public-service organizations. It's not just the incredible obsession we all have today with immediacy – for a fast return on our investment. It's also that public sector managers manage in a fishbowl. The public and media watch, without understanding the difficulties of managing change. If something dramatically negative happens during the lag period – in correctional services, for example, if a notorious inmate were to escape – it will inevitably be blamed on "all this change nonsense." The whole process can easily be aborted at that point.

Ironically, the private sector has it easier in such situations. A company facing a cash flow problem can suspend paying dividends to its shareholders for a quarter, but a government can't suspend welfare cheques for three months. Nothing prevents a company from planning two years of losses on a certain product if the board of directors and the shareholders decide accordingly. On the other hand, it is very difficult for a minister to tell the country: "We are going to pollute the environment a little more than in the past because we are making changes to our environment ministry, but don't worry because in two years it will be better than before." That just won't fly. Or imagine in corrections, the minister announcing: "You will see a few more prisoners escaping than in the past and committing a few more serious offenses. But don't worry, we're on the right track. We're planning for that – it's all part of a long-term improvement scheme." So it takes a little luck as well as a lot of determination to overcome the conservatism of nature. There is no quick fix, no easy way.

AGENCIES THAT CHAMPION CHANGE

Some countries overcome the conservatism of nature by establishing agencies to serve as Change Champions. Malta's Management Systems Unit Ltd. is a limited liability company wholly owned by the government that was established as a catalyst for change on the advice of a reform commission. The agency helps to transform the public service in areas such as leadership, strategy, quality of work life, and information technology. It operates along the lines of a commercial company and is not subject to public service regulations. The unit's operations are publicly scrutinized by the Parliamentary Public Accounts Committee and its business plan is submitted each year to the House of Representatives.

"A complex relationship was created by the fact that Malta Systems Unit is outside the public service but works with public servants," reports Joe Brincat, the consultant who replied to our questionnaire. "The reform process takes place alongside the ordinary administrative running of the public service and not independently of it. It is easy to forget this fact and assume the same commitment and enthusiasm on the part of people who are forced to deal with the more immediate day-to-day problems."

Indeed, civil servants were so preoccupied with their own daily problems that the reform agenda was relegated to a low place on their priorities list. That led to a loss of focus. "There was an exaggerated reliance on Malta Systems Unit to deal with the change process, resulting in an abdication of managerial responsibility on the part of the public service," he notes.

The Egyptian Management Development Center for Industry is mandated to develop the country's future managers in the government and entrepreneurial sectors. Mohamed Hussein, director leads "by asking questions."

Egypt's Cabinet Information and Decision Support Centre was established in 1985 to champion change in information technology. The center signs agreements with various ministries to oversee

the introduction of information technology initiatives but its goal
is to hand day-to-day system operations back to the department,
which might then choose to hire private sector help. "We work as
a consultant rather than an implementer. We out-source. That
helps to build the information technology industry in Egypt, which
is one of our goals," says Vice-Chair Ahmed Nazif. "We see ourselves as stimulating and encouraging. Then we let the market take
over."

One of the keys to success for the agency was early victories.
That developed high credibility for the center. "When you establish
a strong reputation it becomes easier to do things," says Nazif.

Muskogee Veterans Benefits also found early successes vital in
countering skepticism and encouraging buy-in to its transformation
initiative. "Each change became a building block of success. Now
employees take pride in the many visitors from other government
agencies that come to visit," says Vicky Wilcoxen, the Total Quality Control coordinator.

Change, she stresses, must become an ally – a point made by several of our well-performing organizations. "You make people see
the change ends up being for their own benefit even if there is initial discomfort. People now realize here that there will be overall
benefits to change. It becomes a better place for them to work," she
says. "We still get the initial 'Oh my God, here we go again!' But
the change curve is not as steep as it was. There is a certain trust
because of our track record."

David Mee of Ontario's transportation ministry contends that if
managers help people to become comfortable with change, they will
adapt, seeing it as an opportunity. He notes that organizations often
divide people into survivors and casualties of change, the survivors
being those who managed to get through a restructuring without
any change to their lot while the casualties are those declared surplus. He believes it's actually the reverse and organizations must
come to realize that. The casualties are actually those who don't
change and the survivors are those who can bounce with change
and adjust. "They have to get comfortable with the discomfort and
look at it as an opportunity," he says. "And it's management's role
to encourage such thinking and provide the support. Often it takes
professional help, people who can talk to them about change and
turning risk into an opportunity, both in their work and personal
life."

THE YEAR OF THE MINISTRY

When Richard Nottage was on a ten-week sabbatical at Oxford in the fall of 1994, the foreign affairs and trade secretary realized that, like him, the ministry needed a time out for reflection and renewal after the wrenching changes New Zealand had experienced in the previous decade. "I was concerned with how you preserve a high-performing organization amidst the change – there were more responsibilities on the ministry, yet less people and less money. The place was creaking a bit," he recalls.

So he declared a Year of the Ministry, in which foreign affairs and trade would take time to look at itself. Staff were surveyed to determine their concerns, with pay emerging as the greatest irritant. Committees were established to study everything from mission to people policies. Some policy mechanisms have since been tweaked, certain irksome administrative routines were eliminated, and new personnel initiatives, such as subsidizing gym memberships, were introduced. "It was profoundly helpful for morale. It was getting ownership of the process by employees," Nottage says of the effort. "The place had a flat feel before. There's now a sense of social cohesion and even fun. You have to do this every three or four years."

Denmark's industrial injuries board transformed its workplace from a routine operation – "Think Henry Ford," says Information Technology Chief Marianne Hvolris – to a system in which each staff member takes responsibility for all aspects of a case. Since that offered more self-actualization, it might be expected to be well-received, but it was a revolutionary change and naturally spawned insecurities. Employees simply didn't know if they could handle the new challenges. The agency concentrated on education and a supportive environment to smooth the way. "They have adapted. Most of them now feel it's worth the anxiety because they have the job enrichment," says Hvolris.

We've seen that in our own workplace, as correctional officers who never interacted with inmates and in some cases had low literacy skills were asked to take responsibility for case work. They would now have to enter and retrieve data on a computer and become counselors and advisors to inmates, as well as performing their traditional security duties. Managers in such cases have to be sensitive to the disruptions it causes – on and off the job. Employees have to be supported through all the steps.

At the same time, managers in all organizations have to be skeptical when they are repeatedly told by staff that "we've had enough change; we need to slow down and catch our breath." Sometimes that's true: it's a logical time to consolidate and rethink, to have a Year of the Ministry. But more often than not it's just a plea to our humanity by people who are intrinsically against change and unwilling to learn new habits. We're tempted to slow down to be nice to them. But if you've developed trust, learning, and teamwork, then change will be easier to live with and you can keep pushing ahead.

At the same time that managers push ahead, they must ensure they are carving out sufficient time in their own frenetic lives for reflection. This is terribly difficult to accomplish unless you are very disciplined. Organizations will absorb all of the time you make available to them – and then some. But good leaders must recharge their batteries and ponder how the organization is faring in its mission.

A colleague once told us that a deputy minister should only have two things on his desk: his right boot and his left boot. That's an exaggeration, but it holds an important lesson. Leaders must take time to reflect about matters. And that can be difficult in a world where attending meetings and writing memos is considered more important than thinking. Barbara Moses writes about a manager who, when he is in his office thinking, protects himself by placing his hands over the computer keyboard so passersby will realize he's actually working. Clearly we have to be more generous about reflection and accept that it is indeed work – important work.

CHANGE IS MESSY

The textbooks don't tell you that change is messy, no matter how potent the planning or how elegant the model. Our agencies had good diagnosis, good planning, and good implementation. Without that, the process would have been a disaster. With them, mistakes still arise – things that need to be gone over again and corrected. We saw a remarkable honesty in replies describing what can go wrong. We also saw a willingness to admit to mistakes, to change course, without changing destination. Major change is inevitably mismanaged: there are always unintended negative effects on staff and service. But rather than being the agency's downfall, these situations are noticed and dealt with. They become an opportunity to demonstrate the character and skill of the organization.

CHANGE MODELS

There was more variety in the approach to change than to some other topics. Nonetheless, many in our sample had a change management model that helped guide them through the process.

They recognized the need for a tool, but chose different tools to fit their needs. The model mentioned by a couple of respondents, and one we use is that proposed by Harvard University's John Kotter (see Figure 11.1).

John Kotter on Leading Change

In his book *Leading Change*, John Kotter outlines an eight-step process for creating major change.

1 Establish a sense of urgency
2 Create the guiding coalition
3 Develop a vision and strategy
4 Communicate the change vision
5 Empower broad-based action
6 Generate short-term wins
7 Consolidate gains and produce more change
8 Anchor the new changes in the culture

Figure 11.1

CREATIVE FUNDING

Illustrating how they used change to adjust to the environment while focusing on their aim, some respondents got into creative funding. Virtually every agency in our survey had responded to fiscal restraint measures by reducing expenses. Some voluntarily went further, seeking creative ways to increase income. RCMP signed a marketing deal with Disney Productions for the exclusive right to market the lucrative RCMP image, in exchange for royalties which are used to supplement the RCMP budget. In Costa Rica, the Public Service Commission barters its consulting services in exchange for equipment, furnishings, and materials. The Mexican Telefonica is increasing its revenues to reduce its dependence on government support. Creative ways are being devised to help cope with fiscal pressures.

CHAMPIONING CHANGE

Well-performing organizations constantly change and improve. Both they and their more poorly performing cousins live in a world of change. The main difference between the two seems to be that the effective agencies have built a framework of trust, truth, openness, communication, and continuous learning that allows them to steer their own internal change agenda and ease the burden of externally imposed change. Change management has not, historically, been an attribute of the public service. It is now a necessity. Everyone must be a Change Champion.

CAPSULES

- New Brunswick Human Resources Development used Change Champions as an intermediary between top management and front-line staff during a workplace transformation.
- Two decades ago, government bureaucracies were structured so that buffers prevented change. Managers didn't have to be change agents. Today, for our well-performing organizations, managing change is a requred skill for public-service administrators.
- It's important for managers to study the contours of change, because it appears in different forms and with differing force and frequency.
- Our study unearthed three useful ways of delineating change.

  1 The first is by size. Some change is massive, hitting the organization after a wide-ranging reassessment. On other occasions, change is incremental, the continuous improvement and continuous adjustment of an organization navigating towards its North Star or Southern Cross.
  2 Change can also be characterized by the degree to which it is externally or internally propelled. It falls into three categories:

    i   primarily internal change, driven by continuous improvement or strategic initiatives in an effort to improve service and reduce cost;

   ii externally driven change in which the organization can strategically determining how to respond;

  iii environmental change, driven externally by the effects of technology and globalization.

3 The third way of looking at change could best be described as good change or bad change: good change is in harmony with the mandate and allows the organization to better achieve its goals, while bad change is at cross-purposes with the mandate.

- In managing change, all of the other attributes of public service management we have been exploring become vital. But two exceed all the others in importance: mission and people.
- Change might be a talisman of success for managers, but it can appear to be a harbinger of doom for their staff. Our well-performing organizations are aware of that danger and stressed it much more than we've seen in any text on change management.
- Saskatchewan Highways and Transportation pointed out that the bulk of employees hit by organizational change experience the grief cycle made famous by Elisabeth Kubler-Ross in her work on death and dying.
- To help cope with change, many of our respondents provide training in the nature of change and how to manage its impact on the individual.
- It's important to wipe away the image we all carry of Big Bang change, managers creating a new universe in one fiery moment of redefinition. In fact, the conservatism of nature principle suggests that the first six to eight months of a major restructuring will see little progress – and it can be an explosive and dangerous time, if managers are not alert and lucky.
- One of the keys to success in a change process is early victories.
- Managers must help employees to see change as an ally – to help them understand that change will end up being for their benefit as the agency becomes a better place to work.
- In most cases, managers must ignore pleas to slow down or pause. But sometimes it's wise to take a Year of the Ministry.

- Leaders must ensure they are carving out sufficient time in their own frenetic lives for reflection.
- Change management has not, historically, been an attribute of the public service. It is now a necessity. Everyone must be Change Champions.

EXPLORATIONS

In our survey we asked: *How much attention has been paid to a broad-based understanding of the process of change in your organization? What is likely to happen – how are people likely to react – during periods of change? How do you ensure that change becomes the way of life in your organization and what do you do to ensure that your organization stays the course?*

To what extent does your organization see change as a way of life? To what extent is it willing to rethink everything it does in a fundamental way to improve its performance continually and/or adapt to significantly different circumstances?

Other questions that might be useful include:

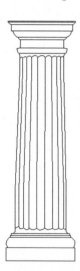

What change management principles does your organization use?

What new ones might be useful to add?

How could they best be introduced?

CHAPTER 12

Final Thoughts

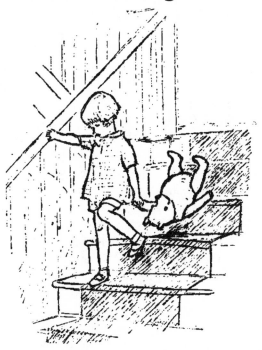

A.A. Milne, in *Winnie the Pooh*,[1] writes: "Here is Edward Bear, coming downstairs now, bump, bump, bump, on the back of his head, behind Christopher Robin. It is, as far as he knows, the only way of coming downstairs, but, sometimes, he feels that there really is another way. If only he could stop bumping for a moment and think of it."

At one time or another, most public servants have felt like Winnie. And the poorly performing agencies that we all know seem, like Winnie, doomed to repeat that experience daily. But there *is* another way, as our well-performing agencies have shown.

It is our belief that public servants – and public service organizations can stop bumping.

The alternative to bump,

        bump,

                bump,

                        is aim, character, and execution. Those three pillars aren't easy to construct. But by applying a Socratic approach, and sufficient discipline, people can invigorate their own workplace through the lessons learned from our well-performing organizations. The success stories we have reported demonstrate that character and dedication to a goal can forge impressive results. They illustrate what it is like to stop bumping and think of a better way.

That a better way exists is too often ignored – by public servants and by their critics. In 1930, French Prime Minister André Pierre Tardieu wrote that "if someone wishes to earn applause, he need only talk about reforming the public service ... no one knows what it means." Today, to earn applause, one need only criticize the public service ... no one would come to their defense.

With that in mind, in this final chapter we'd like to touch on a few of the broader issues affecting the public service as well as address some ancillary matters that cropped up in the study but have not been dealt with fully in other chapters. To begin: it is time to stop defaming the public service. Done well, the public service is the best, most efficient, and most effective way to meet social needs. And every society must address social needs.

Instead of public-service bashing, we should be looking at how to raise the bar – how to make government more government-like, more true to itself, and how to make poorly performing agencies more like their well-performing counterparts. Just as we sometimes wish there were mechanisms equivalent to bankruptcy that would clear up the clutter in the public sector, we sometimes wish there were mechanisms similar to the auditor general to shed light on some private sector operations. Instead of rolling grenades into the hallways, and yelling, "Incoming! Private sector management!" we should be developing and sharing information about the best practices between the public and the private sector. We should also be asking the private sector to adapt some of the better, nobler principles of the public sector, and to work together to improve the economic and social condition of each country.

Herbert Simon, one of the grand old men of management theory – Nobel Prize winner, economist, and early contributor to the field of artificial intelligence – recently observed.[2]

- There is no evidence that the private sector is better than the public sector. The best of the public service is as good as the best of the private sector, and the worst of each is also hard to distinguish between. The media concentrates on the best of the private sector, and the worst of the public sector.
- Power in society needs to be dispersed.[3] Any economic oligarchy will lead to a political oligarchy. We need the balance of government, private sector, and non-government, non-profit, and volunteer organizations to balance society, and to balance power.
- At the core of the "make government more like the private sector" school is a false motivational premise – that public servants act solely in their own self interest. In fact, people act partly in self interest, and partly out of loyalty to and interest in their groups. The "invisible hand" conjured up by Adam Smith is not solely the invisible hand of the profit motive.

WHAT THE PUBLIC SECTOR CAN LEARN FROM THE PRIVATE SECTOR

The public sector can learn much from the private sector. At the government-wide level, "Re-inventing Government" and the "New Public Management" are leading to improvements. Successes due to use of these techniques have been attained in several countries. Specific private sector management tools, such as the concepts of organizational lifecycle, innovation, customer satisfaction, and efficiency, can help. But we caution that each must be applied with a recognition that the nature of the public service, and the background of the particular organization, will require that the approach be modified somewhat for optimal transfer.

WHAT THE PRIVATE SECTOR CAN LEARN FROM THE PUBLIC SECTOR

In the private sector, too many people, for too long, have subscribed to the libertarian school of thought: seek to maximize profit, power, and personal gain, even at the expense of others. They have much to learn about multiple goals. Our favorite private sector book, *Built to Last*,[4] describes several enormously successful American companies that have adopted multiple goals. They have established a mission, a long-term contribution to society, while simultaneously, but secondarily, turning a good profit, and building an organization to last. ServiceMaster CEO Bill Pollard[5] describes how they achieve profitability and pursue excellence as a *means* to achieve the *end* goals of helping people develop and honoring God.

Without fully recognizing that their work overlaps what is already happening in the best of the public sector, several popular writers are pursuing similar themes. James Redfield, in *The Celestine Prophesy*[6] and *The Tenth Insight*,[7] foresees a society where the mission of private sector firms must involve a higher awareness. He sees a progression: "Our questions must change. Instead of asking what product or service I can develop to make the most money, we're beginning to ask, 'What can I produce that liberates and informs and makes the world a better place, yet also preserves a delicate environmental balance?'" Redfield sees "enlightened capitalism" following a new ethic of reducing prices, to help nudge the economy and society in the preferred direction, rather than just focusing on personal gain.

The private sector can also learn from the management strengths of the public sector. Companies have been raiding well-performing public service organizations, including the ones in our sample, to find leaders. Jocelyn Bourgon, clerk of the Privy Council (Canada's chief civil servant), has noted: "The private sector used to be in production; we were in the management of information. They were in manufacturing; we were managing networks. They were in processing; we were managing strategic alliances and consensus building. Today, they are in the service sector. They are managing networks. They are managing conflicting objectives. We have always been doing those things. We are the best trained work force in the country for dealing with issues of that type."

PRIVATIZATION

We did not, in our research, study privatization. The topic received little attention in the responses to our survey. It was not one of the major strategies of well-performing public service agencies. But it needs to be discussed, given the frenzy for privatization in certain quarters. There are definitely some benefits accruing from privatization – and some drawbacks as well. The balancing of the two often gets submerged in the almost crusade-like zeal with which each side advocates its position.

The research on privatization is mixed. More recent meta-research is teasing out that privatization is successful under some conditions yet ineffective in others. Graeme Hodge and E.W. Russell, professors of management in Australia, have looked extensively at the international experience.[8] Reviewing over 129 studies, they found that privatization works well in specific areas, such as garbage collection and cleaning and maintenance, but not as well in policy matters and services where there are competing priorities.

We would suggest it's important to add to those findings the argument advanced by Herbert Simon, Henry Mintzberg, Peter Drucker, and demonstrated in our research study, that the best of the public service can definitely go head-to-head with the best of the private sector. That deflates much of the ideological fervor for privatization. At the same time, we are also concerned that the worst of the public sector rivals the worst of the private sector. At times, one wishes mechanisms were available equivalent to bankruptcy that would clear up the clutter in the public sector. It is easier for a bad operation to keep chugging along in the public sector.

We also believe it is critical that the notion of life cycle be inserted into this debate. Countries at different points in their economic and social development will need different things from their public service and, therefore, different types of public service. It follows that at different stages in their evolution countries will require different degrees of privatization. One model does not fit all countries for all time.

Finally, balance is needed, as both Simon and Mintzberg urge. We have witnessed the damage caused when the state drives out the private sector, as in the communist countries. We have seen societies fail to thrive when they lack a strong third sector of non-profit, volunteer organizations. And we have seen the realization of Lord Acton's dictum, that absolute power corrupts absolutely, in countries where the private sector is unchecked by a solid government and unbalanced by a thriving third sector.

CUSTOMER SATISFACTION

Another popular theme that we did not specifically address in our questionnaire was customer satisfaction. Virtually every respondent, however, stressed the need to focus on customer satisfaction, either raising it in response to our final question about additional factors we may have missed, or weaving it into replies on other questions. Significantly, many agencies connected it to mission. The essence of their organization was to have a positive impact on society and to improve the lot of individuals. Agencies recognized, throughout their responses to our survey, the importance of treating customers with dignity and good manners in a fair, accessible, and responsive manner.

"Legendary Service" is Manitoba Agriculture's creed. Every employee is trained in superior service. Their "think smart" approach encourages staff to come forward with suggestions to improve service. And they weren't alone, as the examples in this book have shown repeatedly, from Muskogee Veterans Benefits trying to make the language on its forms clearly understood to the Norwegian Petroleum Directorate locating near the oil industry.

At the same time, it's important to recognize again that the relationship between citizens and public service – government and its customers – is much more complicated than the relationship between private-sector companies and their customers. New Brunswick's Human Resources Development Ministry had to clarify that its ultimate customer was the taxpayer, not the people flocking to its office. At the same time, however, it also diligently worked to improve the speed of service to the clients directly using the service and also to dramatically heighten its ability to turn those individuals' lives around.

The Swiss Environment, Forests, and Landscape Board stresses that "environmental protection is everyone's business; the entire community has to act responsibly. All community members have to be aware of the impact of their actions and deeds on the environment." Each citizen interacts with the environment daily, and is responsible for helping to preserve the environment. More than a customer, they are partners in preserving the environment.

At the other extreme, the United States Defense Armaments Research Group did not share its results with the public nor seek public input. But the agency did focus quite successfully (as the world found out during the Gulf War) on meeting the needs of its more direct customer – the U.S. military.

Between those two poles lie some public services where totally pleasing the customer at the wicket is virtually impossible. The two revenue agencies in our sample don't try to please the customer by not collecting taxes. Instead, they try to be as polite, efficient, and fair-minded as possible – to earn respect and to be trusted. And in some cases, different customers for the same service demand opposite results, so you cannot possibly satisfy both. In the world of foreign affairs, France wanted its ally, New Zealand, to ignore the resumption of nuclear testing in the South Pacific. Australia wanted its ally, New Zealand, to protest and try to stop the testing. How could New Zealand satisfy both allies, or "customers"?

The focus of public servants is not so much on *satisfying* customers as on achieving the mission. Through focusing on achieving the mission, citizen satisfaction comes as a natural consequence. The values of well-performing public service agencies require them to relate to the citizen in a polite, gracious, fair manner. Even citizens who fail to get what they want – a denied construction permit, for example – should be able to leave the transaction knowing they have been dealt with fairly and that the agency dealt with is accomplishing something worthwhile.

And let us not forget that private sector customer satisfaction is not always top-notch. Which of us does not have a horror story about false advertising, hidden defects, rude clerks, inadequate refund and repair policies, price gouging, and crass self-interest in dealings with the private sector? Many newspapers have popular columns in which a reporter investigates customer grievances about private sector companies. They tend to find the same group of private sector companies get complained about while another group receives the praise. So it is with the public sector. Some agencies generate a lot of complaints; others generate a lot of compliments. Typically, the media looks at the former. This book examines the latter.

DEVELOPING NATIONS

Throughout our research, we were concerned about the need to avoid presenting solely a first world model. The countries in our research* are at different levels of development, yet deal with

---

* Australia, Canada, Costa Rica, Denmark, Egypt, Lebanon, Malta, Mexico, New Zealand, Norway, Philippines, Singapore, Switzerland, United States of America

remarkably similar issues and respect remarkably similar principles. We supplemented our research by working with the United Nations Division of Governance, Public Administration, and Finance. That group convened a meeting of international experts to review the applicability of our approach to developing nations.

A.T.R. Rahman, former deputy director of the U.N. division, reminds us that "as apples cannot grow in a warm climate, similarly systems and practices rooted in one type of culture have limited scope for transferability in a different cultural context." Indeed a farmer in a low-income country, clawing away at the soil by hand and hoe, cannot be expected to use the same tools as a large corporate farm in North America, with its million-dollar, eight-wheel-drive, air-conditioned tractor with stereo system. But both are subject to the same laws of farming. You reap what you sow. You prepare the soil before you plant. You need water and warmth for plants to grow. Certain principles are shared, despite the many differences in culture and tools.

Participants at our meeting from third world countries pointed out that an effective public service requires some stability of government as a precondition, and a critical mass of public servants with competence, character, and commitment. In many developing countries, the issue is to build such capacity from scratch – or, worse, from a historic base of corruption, discontinuity, and self-serving interests. In some countries people's interest is focused on basic survival, or on the next coup, or on the bullets whizzing past their ears. In such cases, the tranquillity of a Socratic dialogue, and the three pillars, seem like distant dreams.

But it is dreams that people strive for. And what we heard from our colleagues in developing countries was that these pillars – these areas of focus – may well be helpful in guiding the design of early initiatives. They also noted that the approach of asking questions allows them to develop their own approach to suit their climate and specific situation, while respecting the universal principles that lie behind good government and effective public service. The principles of good public service, like the laws of the farm, are universal.

We described four conditions that appear common across our survey, that are driving public sector reform: fiscal pressures, changing citizen expectations, working in a fishbowl, massive global change. Rahman notes that developing countries face additional pressures: "Unstable political environments caused by civil and political unrest; dealing with tribal, ethnic, linguistic, and religious divisions; initiating a democratic system and maintaining the integrity and fairness of an electoral system; finding agreement on a political and governance framework as embodied in a constitutional and legal framework; preventing politicians and their collaborating civil servants from misappropriating and stealing public treasury and development grants and loans; and ex-communist countries grappling with the problems of building economic infrastructures for introducing a market economy." Some of those public services are without the pressures of transparency and public participation that fuel good service in the developed countries. In some developing or undeveloped countries, the public voices its concerns about the quality and speed of service only at risk of imprisonment, and copes with access through use of bribes.

Quite a challenge. A challenge that has been faced at one time or another by many countries that have made the transformation to good government.

It's worth remembering that a century ago the now-developed nations grappled with integrity in public service. Turn-of-the-century North America was not an ideal place. Nor was Australia in the days of forced population by convicts. Others in our sample have recently gone through civil war. In various countries politicians were often corrupt, organized crime had an influence, nepotism was rampant. In reaction, reformers established complex laws and procedures to reduce these abuses.

Given the seemingly insurmountable obstacles to transforming a whole society all at once, it may be that there is a role in developing nations for individuals, groups, and agencies to use the three pillars, and the dialogue approach, as a starting point for local change.

DEMOCRACY

One of the challenges many nations face is how to build a democracy, or to strengthen the democratic system they have. Democracy is more than one person, one vote. As agencies do with their mission statement, countries state their values in their constitution. Just as there is a universal mission statement for public agencies, there appears to be a universal mission statement for democratic countries. By implementing those democratic values within individual agencies, by entrenching them within the behavior of individuals, the agency contributes to the growth of democracy. In a very real sense, democracy is the embodiment at the national level of some of the same principles that drive good performance at the agency level. Openness and transparency. Truth and trust. Continuous learning. The more these skills, and characteristics, are built at the local level, the more they can contribute to growth at the national level. The more an employee is able to accept delegation of authority, be seen as accountable, and act in the best interest of the mission, the more easily the citizen will be able to accept delegation of authority to elect the government, to hold them accountable, and to continue to act in the best interest of their nation.

A well-performing public service is essential to the growth, development, and maintenance of both an effective government and a thriving private sector.

A public service agency that builds the three pillars also builds support for democracy and the country's values. They model the right behavior, and social learning is one of the principal ways adults learn. By practising delegation, networking, etc., they build those skills so essential for a mature democracy. By leading beyond their borders, they share those skills with others. The Philippines Development Bank has made this a clear strategy (see chapter 3). Nations seeking to strengthen their democracy might want to ask if applying the Three Pillars would help them on their journey.

HOW TO USE THIS BOOK

This book was written in the hope that it would help public servants to improve their performance and thereby better serve their governments and their citizens. We have endeavored to make the book easy to read and accessible, particularly so that we could reach and assist those public servants who have an obligation to look for opportunities to improve performance but who are always terribly busy – supervisors at all levels, from the first-line supervisor to the most senior civil servant. We also hope that students of management, and consultants who advise managers, will be able to develop a better understanding of their subject through a question-based approach to their future work. All of them should find something of value in this book. It is hoped they will use it as intended: as a respectful way of calling forth the talents and insights that can be found in all corners of public service around the globe.

As the reader will appreciate, we have used prescriptions very sparingly. Instead, we have tapped into some questions that some particularly well-performing organizations seem to have wrestled with as they became well-performing and that they continue to wrestle with as they maintain their quest for excellence.

We believe that those questions could be useful for other organizations to consider and debate as well. We have found that both managers and employees respond much more positively to such an approach than the more typical, prescriptive, "Here is what you have to do" pattern. The questioning model builds on the creativity, intelligence, and organizational knowledge of employees rather than assuming that an outsider knows better than those who actually "wear the shoes." The questioning model is also less threatening as it delegates responsibility for diagnosis and action to employees and their managers.

It is not a panacea, the one management tool that will see you through to success. But it is a way of understanding. Socrates used to ask his students, and public officials, questions that challenged their assumptions, their way of doing things, their basic understanding. It often left them uncomfortable, with more questions than answers, but it opened the path to new learning.

Others are also reviving this approach. Lance Secretan, in *Reclaiming Higher Ground*,[9] notes that managers are "well experienced in providing answers, but it is likely that we have enough (answers). It seems to me that our greater challenge is to ask the right questions. This is not easy, because although an expert maintains an inventory of answers, there is no inventory of questions. Knowing and remembering to ask the right questions requires wisdom and judgment."

In asking those questions, it's helpful to follow the advice of Albert Edward Day:[10]

Humble questioning is the recognition that one does not know it all.
Sincere questioning is genuine hospitality to another's viewpoint.
Brave questioning means a willingness to be disturbed mentally, morally, and spiritually.
Intelligent questioning witnesses to a conviction that only in another's answers may lie salvation from absurdity.

Or, as Socrates put it: "The unexamined life is not worth living."

People learn and gain inspiration in a myriad of ways, so it would be foolish to present a single plan for implementing the ideas in the book. But in following Socrates and examining organizational life, supervisors might like to explain to their employees some general features of our model and then invite them to brainstorm with some of the "Explorations." We suggest not rushing through too many of the questions in one session. It seems better to allow people to think through the process, using one or two questions to illustrate the procedure. It is very important that everyone feel comfortable and not forced to make up their mind about issues that they have had little or no time to consider, using a process that they may be uncertain about. If the pace is kept moderate enough for the whole group, the payoff will be larger and, over the long-term, the pace will actually be quicker. Remember: this is not a quick fix approach to improvement!

We suspect it will be important to take solid notes during the discussion of individual questions or examples. Good ideas should be captured as they spring to mind; otherwise they fall victim to our fallible memories.

As ideas and workable responses pile up, we suggest that they be revisited from time to time. An idea often looks better when it takes its place among the other worthwhile ideas. As well, an idea that gleams appealingly at first sight may loose its lustre when subject to questioning and placed in its proper context.

For these reasons, we suggest that you look at each set of questions on an area together (for instance, mission), adding ones you think would be useful. When you have material for an overarching theme (such as aim), you might review the whole group of questions and responses to ensure that what you have assembled is coherent and suitable for your organization. That same review procedure might be followed when all the sections of the book have been explored and a broader vision has emerged for consideration.

Finally, we should warn you that once you have started execution in a serious manner, you will need to revisit both questions and responses on a regular basis. Dialogue is not a one-time fad but a habit. Things change. Challenges change, conditions change, ideas change, and we, as individuals, change. It is also our experience that as people get into the habit of thinking systematically about their work and how to improve it, they become better and better at it. So keep revisiting the same questions and inventing some other ones that unlock the path of discovery for you. And don't forget to have fun as you undertake this serious exercise of supporting our citizens and governments better.

From the start, we have recognized that this is preliminary work. It is not finished – like the agencies we studied, we recognize the need for continuous improvement. Please share your experiences with us, so that we may learn from you.

CAPSULES

- The alternative to bump, bump, bump is aim, character, and execution. By applying a Socratic approach, and sufficient discipline, people can invigorate their own workplace through the lessons learned from our well-performing organizations.
- Instead of public-service bashing, we should be looking at how to raise the bar – how to make government more government-like, and how to make poorly performing agencies more like their well-performing counterparts.
- Herbert Simon tells us of the need for a balance of government, private sector, and non-government, non-profit, and volunteer organizations to balance society and to balance power.
- At the core of the "make government more like the private sector" school is a false motivational premise – that public servants act solely in their own self interest.
- The public sector has much to learn from the private sector. But the private sector can learn from the public sector, notably on managing multiple goals.
- There are definitely some benefits accruing from privatization – and some drawbacks as well. The balancing of the two often gets disturbed in the almost crusade-like zeal with which each side advocates its position.
- We are concerned that the worst of the public sector rivals the worst of the private sector. At times, one wishes mechanisms were available equivalent to bankruptcy that would clear up the clutter in the public sector.
- It is critical that the notion of life cycle be inserted into the privatization debate. Countries at different points in their economic and social development will need different things from their public service and, therefore, different types of public service.

- Virtually every respondent to our survey stressed the need to focus on customer satisfaction.
- It's important to recognize that the relationship between citizens and public service – government and its customers – is much more complicated than the relationship between private-sector companies and their customers.
- The focus of public servants is not so much on *satisfying* customers as on *achieving* the mission.
- Participants at our meeting with third world countries pointed out that good public service requires some stability of government as a precondition, and a critical mass of public servants with competence, character, and commitment. In many developing countries, the issue is to build such capacity from scratch – or, worse, from a historic base of corruption, discontinuity, and self-serving interests.
- What we heard, however, from our colleagues in developing countries was that the three pillars may well be helpful in guiding the design of early improvement initiatives. They also noted that the approach of asking questions allows them to develop their own approach to suit their climate and specific situation, while respecting the universal principles that lie behind good government and effective public service.

Humble questioning is the recognition that one does not know it all.
Sincere questioning is genuine hospitality to another's viewpoint.
Brave questioning means a willingness to be disturbed mentally, morally, and spiritually.
Intelligent questioning witnesses to a conviction that only in another's answers may lie salvation from absurdity.

A.E. Day

- Supervisors might like to explain some of the general features of our model to their employees and then invite them to brainstorm with some of the Explorations.
- As ideas and workable responses pile up, we suggest that they be revisited from time to time. An idea often looks better when it takes its place among the other worthwhile ideas. As well, an idea that looks quite appealing when it stands alone may look less attractive when placed in its proper context and subject to questioning.

- We suggest that you look at each set of questions on an attribute together and, when you have material for an overarching theme, review the whole group of questions and responses to ensure that what you have assembled is coherent and right for your organization. The same procedure might be followed when all the sections of the book have been explored and you have developed a broader vision for consideration,
- Finally, we should warn you that once you have started execution in a serious manner, you will probably need to revisit both questions and responses on a regular basis. Dialogue is a habit not a fad..
- And yes, we really would like to hear from you.

If you would like to contact the authors, you can do so at the following address:

Ole Ingstrup, Commissioner
or Paul Crookall
Correctional Services of Canada
340 Laurier Avenue West
Ottawa, Ontario, Canada
K1A 0P9
or by E-mail: *pcrookal@magi.com*

Explorations

During our study, we asked questions to build our understanding of effective public service. At the end of each chapter, we have listed these questions, plus others that we think might be helpful in better understanding how to improve public service.

Good managers realize their wisdom comes from knowing their own ignorance and therefore asking a lot of questions.

It's also a style we have brought to this book. It would be easy to claim we have found some instant formula for managerial success: nine miracle ingredients that form three crucial pillars. Life isn't that simple, however. Instead, we believe our findings have to be viewed as a starting point for explorations rather than as an end point. Our nine attributes are not a checklist of guaranteed solutions but rather a checklist of important questions that leaders of well-performing institutions seem to ask — and that we feel others would be wise to apply to their own agencies.

Here we summarize those questions.

As you look through them and think about them, we ask that you:

1   Relax. It's not a test. Think about your organization, and your contribution to it. Dig deep into your heart, your soul, your mind, to find the answers.
2   Stretch. Use BHAG thinking (Big Hairy Audacious Goals). Think of Margaret Mead's observation: "Never doubt that a small group of thoughtful, committed people can change the world. Indeed, it is the only thing that ever has."
3   Write down your answers in a few words to trigger your subsequent reviews.
4   Talk about these matters with your colleagues.

Questions	Answers
CHAPTER I	
Does your organization perform well?	
What are its best features?	
Which of the nine elements are weak or need improving in your organization?	
Is there a will to improve?	
Might the Socratic method, the ideas in this book, contribute to your efforts?	
What might be some ways to begin the dialogue leading to change?	
Do the poorly performing public service organizations you know have aim, character and execution?	
Do the well performing public service organizations you know have aim, character and execution embedded in a questioning dialogue?	
Who do you talk with about good public management? What questions do you ask?	
*	
*	

* Space is left at the end of question sections so that you can add the questions that you think are important to ask in your own organization.

CHAPTER 3

Does your organization have
a clear mission?

What process would work
best in your organization to
create or improve your mission?

Does your mission speak to
your organization's contribution to society, to its impact
on individuals, to the importance of getting better at
what you do?

Does your mission statement
deal with the mission, core
values, principles, and strategic objectives?

How would you imbed the
mission statement in the character and behavior of the
organization?

Are you building a cathedral,
or pushing paper?

CHAPTER 4

Has your organization
thought carefully about leadership?

How would you describe the
leadership style in your organization?

Is that style consistent with the mission?

Is leadership consistent across the organization?

Have you received feedback on your leadership, its consistency, and its effectiveness?

Do you understand how your leadership contributes to achieving the mission and how you could better contribute?

Is there consistency between word and deed in leadership?

Does the organization take the long view in leadership?

Would the five-step approach to devising a management style be helpful in your organization?

CHAPTER 5

Has your organization properly defined accountabilities?

Are systems in place to monitor achievement of the mission and provide feedback?

Are the right things being measured?

Is recognition practised?	
Are incentives in place for good performance?	
Is bad performance dealt with?	
Do you know where each of your subordinates is on the Results-Values chart? What can you do to move each into the preferred quadrant where they deliver on commitments and live the values?	

CHAPTER 6

Do you feel valued at work?	
What contributes to that feeling?	
What can be done to improve the way people are valued in your organization?	

Chapter 7

Do you have a good understanding of who you need to communicate with, and how well you fare at it?	
Would a bubble chart or its	

equivalent be useful for you personally? For your organization?	
For the people and organizations on your bubble chart, are the expectations clear of how and when you communicate. Of what constitutes quality service?	
How can you manage those expectations?	
Do you have an internal communications plan?	
Do you have an external communications plan?	
What are the strengths and weaknesses of those plans?	
CHAPTER 8	
Can you trust others in your organization?	
Can they trust you?	
Can you speak the truth to those in power?	
Looking at the four types of trust — professional, personal, political, and public — how well is your organization doing?	
What is undermining each kind of trust?	

What can be done to build more trust?	
How open is the organization?	
What can be done to improve openness?	
Is yours a learning organization?	
Are you learning, developing, growing professionally?	
How can the organization better contribute to learning, developing, and improving?	
Five Centuries ago, Machiavelli said "It is better to be feared than to be loved." Is that true today, or is it better to be trusted than to be feared?	
CHAPTER 9	
How long has it been since you inventoried your management tool box. What should be discarded, tuned up, added?	
What problems in your organization need new tools?	
For each problem, what might be some appropriate tools?	

How could you bring the best
tools on-stream in a sensible
fashion?

How do you stay sharp?

CHAPTER 10

Which work in your agency
is better done in teams or by
individuals?

What has been the organization's previous experience
with teams — is it something
to build on, to learn from, or
to avoid?

What model of teamwork
would best suit the situation:
simple, empowered, or self-
directed?

What changes are required to
conform to that model?

Do the mission and values
support teamwork?

Do the leadership and accountability systems promote the
development of teamwork?

Are employees supportive of
teamwork?

What skills are needed for the
people on various teams?

What roadblocks to teams
exist and how can they be
removed?

CHAPTER 11

What change management principles does your organization use?

What new ones might be useful to add?

How could they best be introduced?

APPENDIX B

Question Rankings

We asked each agency to rank each question in our survey as of
high, medium, or lower importance. With 12 questions, we suggested 4 of them be rated as high, 4 as medium, and 4 as low. The
agencies tended to say they were all important, but then complied
with our request to rank them. They did use the "high" rating more
than medium or low. That no doubt reflected the comment of one
respondent: "In my view there is no benefit in ranking the questions
because they are of the same importance and complement each
other." The 12 questions collapsed into nine areas of management
attention, and the 9 areas into 3 pillars.

With those cautions in mind, we present the following overall
rankings as a matter of interest rather than some indication of
importance.

Ranking	Question on	Chapter where discussed
1	Mission	3 Mission (Aim)
2	People	6 People (Character)
3	Communications and relationships	7 Communication (Character)
4	Trust	8 Trust (Character)
5	Accountability	5 Accountability (Aim)
6	Rethinking, improving performance	11 Change Management (Execution)
7	Leadership	4 Leadership (Aim)

Ranking	Question on	Chapter where discussed
8	Understanding and managing change	11 Change (Execution)
9	Networking	4 Communication (Character)
10	Teamwork	10 Teamwork (Execution)
11	Truth, openness, learning from experience	5 Trust (Character)
12	Management tools	9 Management tools (Execution)

One agency, the Manitoba Department of Labour, even told us which questions it thought were inter-related, coming up with three factors very similar to the three pillars that emerged overall. Jim Nykoluk wrote that they were vision (mission, leadership, accountability, networking), the contribution of people (people, communications, trust, teams), and managing change (change, management tools, truth, and learning).

APPENDIX C

Contributors to the Survey

The public service agencies that responded to our survey were:

AUSTRALIA
The Public Service and Merit Protection Commission

CANADA
The National Library
Revenue Canada
The Royal Canadian Mounted Police (RCMP)
Statistics Canada

Canada, Provincial and City Government Organization
The City of Calgary
The City of Toronto
New Brunswick Human Resources Development
The New Brunswick Department of Finance
The Ontario Provincial Police
The Ontario Ministry of Transportation
The Manitoba Department of Agriculture
The Manitoba Department of Labour
The Northwest Territories Workers' Compensation Board
The Nova Scotia Department of Education and Culture
The Nova Scotia Department of Fisheries
The Queen Elizabeth Hospital, Toronto
Saskatchewan Highways and Transportation

COSTA RICA
The Public Service Commission

DENMARK
Arbejdsskadestyrelsen (The National Board of Industrial Injuries)

EGYPT
The Cabinet Information and Decision Support Centre
Management Development Centre for Industry

LEBANON
Civil Service Board

MALTA
Management Systems Unit

MEXICO
Serviccio Publico de Loalizacion Telefonica (Locatel Public Telephone Service)
Instituto Nacional de la Nutricion (Institute of Nutrition)

NEW ZEALAND
Inland Revenue Department
Ministry of Foreign Affairs and Trade

NORWAY
Norwegian Petroleum Directorate

PHILIPPINES
Philippine General Hospital
Development Bank of the Philippines

SINGAPORE
Ministry of Defense
Benevolent Fund Board

SWITZERLAND
Office fédéral de l'environment, des forêts, et du paysage (Ministry of the Environment)
Des services linguistiques centraux (Language Services)
Département fédéral de justice et police (Department of Justice)

UNITED STATES OF AMERICA
U.S. Army Armament Research, Development, and Engineering Center
Defense Mapping Agency, Department of Defense
Department of Veterans' Affairs

Research Method

This appendix describes in more detail the manner in which we conducted the research and wrote the book.

RESEARCH METHOD

The research was conceptualized by Ole Ingstrup when he was principal at the Canadian Centre for Management Development in the early 1990s. It was based on thinking he had done about whether we should be researching for universal *attributes* of well-performing organizations and then trying to emulate those attributes, or whether we should be searching instead for *the right questions* that would lead to better understanding and practice of good public management. His thinking was supplemented through reading and consultation with a wide variety of academics and practitioners from around the world.

The project was further developed at Queen's University in Kingston, Canada, in 1995–96 when Ole was Skelton-Clark Fellow. The precise questions were determined in further consultation with academics and practitioners. The survey was then sent by Jocelyne Bourgon, clerk to the Privy Council (the senior civil servant in Canada, responsible to the prime minister for the public service) to her counterparts in several countries, the ten provinces and two territories of Canada, and two Canadian cities. The letter requested that they "identify two or three sustained, well-performing organizations within your public service (that have) performed at a high level over an extended period (6 to 10 years) and are significant contributors to the public service."

Completed questionnaires were received from about 40% of those contacted. Several others sent letters explaining why they could not participate. A few advised they were interested but, in these busy times, were unable to respond within our time frames. A few others said they had no way of knowing which agencies were long-term, well-performing. A few didn't respond at all – in at least one case, because in their opinion offering two or three nominees would be an insult to the other well-performing agencies which would not be nominated.

We received 40 completed surveys from agencies in 14 countries. The responses were in most cases lengthy, well thought-out, and completed by a senior manager, often with input from teams. A typical response would be about 20 or more pages, with attached reference material. Clearly the responses were not quickly pasted together out of some international politesse. Respondents had devoted considerable time, care, and thought – and some even thanked us for helping them to better understand aspects of their organization through the process of asking and answering questions.

In addition to the narratives, we asked respondents to rate the importance to their organization of each of the twelve areas we queried about. Answers are given in Appendix C. The respondents unanimously agreed that the 12 areas of focus (which we have since condensed to 9 basic areas and three pillars) were absolutely crucial. We asked if we had missed any key areas. About half said no. The other half mentioned issues like customer service and technology, which most of the others had dealt with under the headings of mission and management tools. The consensus was that the 12 areas would grow, rather than decrease, in importance.

Reviewing, understanding, and distilling the voluminous responses became a team effort. The team included the two authors and two research assistants. The responses were first studied by agency, to get a solid understanding of their operations. The responses were next analysed by question, or topic, so that we looked at all the answers on Mission, then all the answers on Leadership, and so on. All of the answers to question one were put in a folder and studied, then another folder for question two, etc. Finally, the answers were put on CD-ROM so that we could key-word search across responses. The review process took about three months – read, think, read again, let it digest, discuss, read, think.

We had started with a few tentative hypotheses and a firm belief that the process of asking questions was a beneficial way not only to learn but also to manage an organization. We did not start with the three pillars in mind – they emerged, quite clearly and quite forcefully, from the data during our review.

We then wrote our findings in a draft paper that was shared with several colleagues, both practitioners and academics. Their consensus was that a very solid and useful model emerged from the data, but more work was needed, and the writing was a little dry.

At that point Harvey Schachter, a respected and experienced journalist, former newspaper editor, and well-known writer on the private sector, joined the team. Harvey interviewed about 25 people from about half the agencies that had responded, to get more of a personal flavor and details, challenge assertions on which we had doubts, and inject a journalistic perspective to complement our academic and practitioner backgrounds.

A revised manuscript resulted, that maintained the three pillars but reduced the 12 areas of focus to 9, while maintaining all of the material from the original 12. Some were collapsed into others (e.g., truth and openness into trust). That manuscript (or papers based on it) was presented at international forums, including the United Nations, the International Institute for Administrative Science, and the American Society for Public Administration.

We then submitted the manuscript to McGill-Queen's University Press, where it was reviewed by their editors and a blind review process by experts in the field.

A qualitative approach was taken to understanding the narratives. We found many things that fit with our understanding of the public service, based on our experience, reading, and consulting. But we also found many new things, which have changed our view of excellence in the public service.

ISSUES

As with most social science research, the research design merits review and could be improved. However, we hasten to point out that, despite its flaws, the design is reasonably advanced in comparison with the "state of the art" as catalogued by Lawrence Lynn Jr. in *Public Management as Art, Science, and Profession.*[1] Unfortunately, that says more about the woeful state of research in public management than it says about the wonderful state of our research. The questions about our research that need to be asked, and answered, follow.

How Were the Survey Data and Our Own Experiences and Opinions Combined (or Kept Separate)?

We have tried, throughout the book, to distinguish what we think from what we distilled from the survey responses and interviews, from what the respondents actually said. That is reflected in the words that we choose to introduce thoughts. We have used extensive quotes from our respondents, in order to use their own words rather than to put our words in their mouths. At the same time, we have some experience as both academics and practitioners, and have something to say from time to time, so we say it but try to be clear that it is our thoughts when we do so.

When our own thoughts and those of the sample are in synch (which is often), we sometimes share our experiences as well. For example, on networking and communications, we share our approach to use of a bubble chart. While none of the respondents mentioned this particular technique, they did stress the importance of having a process to understand and build networks.

After reviewing the data, we decided to present it as we received it – by question. The integrating framework of the three pillars was our understanding of what the respondents told us – it was not a preconceived model and was not even one of our tentative hypotheses. Not only does it fit the data, it has been well-received by many in organizations that were not part of the study, as being relevant to their operations as well.

We started out thinking that the 12 areas of focus that we asked questions about were important and, although interconnected, were conceptually, and to an extent practically, discrete. We figured that while those 12 areas would not be the only ones that managers paid attention to, they would be areas that managers *must* attend to. Failure would impede the potential for success. We ended up, based on the responses, developing the more advanced model presented in the book.

We started out thinking that cultural differences would lead to considerable variation in responses – that the areas to address, such as mission or leadership, would be the same across cultures but that the approaches would be specific to the location. We found far more similarity in responses than we had anticipated.

We started out thinking that the process of asking questions – of engaging in a dialogue – on important organizational issues was a key to success in the public service. We found many others shared our view. John Kotter, for example, in *Leading Change*,[2] argues that "most human beings, especially well-educated ones, buy into something only when they have had a chance to wrestle with it. Wrestling means asking questions, challenging and arguing."

We began with a feeling that most public servants want to make a difference and are not "what's in it for me?" types. They don't want to check their minds, and their souls, at the door on the way in to work. We found that the missions of the organizations we studied met that basic human need, allowing public servants that worked in them to flourish.

And, finally, we began with a belief that sharing success stories and talking about good public management would be beneficial, so we decided to write this book.

How Do We Know the Respondents Are Well-Performing and How Did We Verify the Data?

While it would have been nice to have objective criteria on which to base the selection of agencies, there isn't any. We were forced to accept somebody's advice and for an international study we felt the heads of public services were appropriate choices. By allowing them to nominate several agencies, we also felt we would get a better sample.

We therefore did not reject any nominations of agencies – if the head of the public service was confident in the agency, we accepted that they were in a position to know.

Interestingly, Peters and Waterman employed supposedly objective financial criteria to select their sample for *In Search of Excellence*.[3] They were criticized for their criteria. Moreover, two years later one third of their sample no longer met the criteria for excellence. But the conclusions of the study still provided the basis for much discussion and insight.[4]

Our technique, we found out after we had completed the study, was similar to that used by Collins and Porrasin for *Built to Last*,[5] their best-selling study of the private sector. They asked a sample of chief executives of companies on the Fortune 500 list to nominate the best. We asked the equivalent of the heads of the public sector.

Many of the agencies verified their data themselves. We were impressed that throughout their replies they understood the need for substantiating data, rather than simply providing self-serving rhetoric. Many also mentioned awards they had won, accolades from outside groups, and other evidence of superior performance. In some cases, those accolades are mentioned in the text.

It is important that we do not pretend that every agency we studied is a "world class" performer, although several clearly are that. We asked for the best in the country. Certainly, given the diversity of nations we studied, there will be diversity in "the best" that was presented to us. What was more important to us was that our approach allowed us to reach into countries with less-advanced public services to see if they were subject to the same principles. We learned that they struggled with the same questions and came up with similar answers.

Several of our agencies have experienced major change since the research began. The Australian Public Service Commission has been downsized by half, and is recovering. The Malta Systems Unit has been under review by a new government. The RCMP was criticized in the media over some high-profile cases. The Metro Toronto government has been replaced by a "mega-city" that combined it with other municipalities, and the Defense Mapping Agency has been absorbed into the National Imagery and Mapping Agency.

At the same time as we accepted that the organizations we studied were among the best in their country, we also recognize that each will have its warts and blemishes. Such is the nature of organizations. The important thing is that they appear to have fewer warts and blemishes, achieve more positive outcomes, and learn from their failures – more so than their sister agencies which were not nominated to be in the survey. That some are currently experiencing trauma does not take away from their lengthy record of accomplishments. Nor does it mean that they won't overcome their current challenges.

How Do We Know that What the Agencies Told Us They Do, Is What They Actually Do?

With any self-report, this is a concern. Costa Rica's Civil Service Directorate observed trenchantly at the end of their survey that "today much of the foregoing is a mixture of envisioned objectives and reality in the making." When the RCMP's responses are verified by three independent researchers, and they are ranked as among the best in the world in teamwork and conflict resolution, we are inclined to think they have been honest with us. Not all agencies backed their claims with as thorough documentation. Not all agencies were known to us. Further verification was beyond the scope of this study. We can only report that we found no evidence of over-inflated claims, or misrepresentation.

Why Haven't We Studied Poorly Performing Agencies, to Compare and Contrast?

That was deliberate. Frankly, we've seen enough of them to last a lifetime. And we suspect readers are sufficiently familiar with them to make their own assessments and comparisons. In fact, we encourage the reader to measure poorly performing organizations that they know against the *Three Pillars* model.

In the longer term, however, more research is needed on both the good and the not-so-good in public service organizations.

We recognize our research design is not perfect. But it is broader in the scope of countries and agencies studied, more solid in research design, and more rooted in the experience of practising managers than is much of the previous work in this area. We hope our work will lead to more research, more dialogue, and a better definition of good public service.

Notes

LEARNING FROM THE BEST

1 *Computer World's Global 100*, Framingham, MA: Computer World Inc, May 1, 1995.
2 *Consumer Reports* (Canada), September 1996
3 James Collins and Jerry Porras, *Built to Last: Successful Habits of Visionary Companies* (New York: HarperBusiness, 1994).

STUDYING THE BEST

1 Otto Brodtrick, "Attributes of Well-Performing Organizations." In Auditor General of Canada, *Report to the House of Commons for the Fiscal Year Ended March 31, 1988*, Chapter 4 (Ottawa: Ministry of Supply and Services, 1988).
2 Ibid.
3 Charles Goodsell, *The Case for Bureaucracy: A Public Administration Polemic* (3rd edition) (Chatham, NJ: Chatham House, 1994).
4 David Osborne and Ted Gaebler, *Reinventing Government: How the Entrepreneurial Spirit Is Transforming the Public Sector* (Reading, MA: Addision Wesley, 1992).
5 David Osborne and Peter Plastrik, *Banishing Bureaucracy* (Reading MA: Addison Wesley, 1997).
6 Albert Gore, *The Best Kept Secrets in Government* (Washington, DC: National Performance Review, September 1996).
7 Russell Mills, speech to the Association of Professional Executives of the Public Service of Canada, January 1998, Ottawa.
8 Steven Cohen, *The Effective Public Manager: Achieving Success in Government* (San Franscisco: Jassey-Bass, 1988).

9   James McDavid and Brian Marson, eds., *The Well-Performing Government Organization* (Toronto: Institute of Public Administration of Canada, 1991).

10 Robert Denhardt, *The Pursuit of Significance: Strategies for Managerial Success in Public Organizations* (Belmont: Wadsworth, 1993).

11 CAPAM, *Current Good Practices and New Development in Public Service Management* (Commonwealth Secretariat, 1996). Individual studies on Australia, Malaysia, Malta, New Zealand, and the United Kingdom are also available (phone number in Canada, 1-416-920-3337).

12 Guy Peters and Donald Savoie, eds., *Governance in a Changing Environment* (Montreal: CCMD and McGill-Queen's University Press, 1995).

13 Guy Peters and Donald Savoie, eds., *Taking Stock: Assessing Public Sector Reforms* (Montreal: CCMD and McGill-Queen's University Press, 1998).

14 Christopher Pollitt, "Management Techniques for the Public Sector: Pulpit and Practice." In Peters and Savoie, *Governance in a Changing Environment*, p. 234.

15 Peters and Savoie, *Taking Stock*, p. 5.

16 Allen Schick, The Spirit of Reform: *Managing the New Zealand State Sector in a Time of Change*. Report to the State Services Commission and the Treasury, New Zealand, August 1996, p. 3.

MISSION

1   Stephen Covey, Roger Merrill, and Rebecca Merrill, *First Things First* (New York: Simon and Shuster, 1994), p. 221. (They find in their work "what we've come to call the *universal mission* – 'to improve the economic well-being and quality of life of all stakeholders.'")

2   James Collins and Jerry Porras, *Built to Last: Successful Habits of Visionary Companies.* (New York: HarperBusiness, 1994).

3   These ideas are discussed further in Ole Ingstrup, *Only Those Who Believe Can Stay the Course in Turbulent Times: A Value-based, Strategic Approach to the Management and Development of Corrections* (Ottawa: CCMD, 1995).

LEADERSHIP

1   John Tait, *Discussion Paper on Values and Ethics in the Public Service* (Ottawa: CCMD, December 1996).

2 Patrick L. Townsend and Joan E. Gebhardt, *Five Star Leadership* (New York: John Wiley & Sons, 1997), p. 43–8.

3 Michael Hammer, *Beyond Reengineering* (New York: HarperBusiness, 1996).

4 Michael Hammer and James Champy, *Reengineering the Corporation, A Manifesto for Business Revolution* (New York: HarperBusiness, 1993).

5 Ole Ingstrup, *Public Service Renewal: From Means to Ends* (Ottawa: Canadian Centre for Management Development, 1995).

6 Elliott Jacques, personal interview, and "The Long View of Leadership," *Canadian Business*, May 1992.

7 James Collins and Jerry Porras, *Built to Last: Successful Habits of Visionary Companies* (New York: HarperBusiness, 1994).

8 Bernard Bass, *Leadership and Performance Beyond Expectations* (New York: Free Press, 1985).

ACCOUNTABILITY

1 Robert Behn, *Bottom-Line Government.* (Durham, N.C.: Duke University Governors Center, 1994), p. 19.

2 Ibid.

3 Henry Mintzberg, "Managing Government, Governing Management," *Harvard Business Review* (May–June 1996).

PEOPLE

1 *The Economist*, London, September 7, 1991, p. 88; September 11, 1993, p. 65.

2 Stephen Covey, *Principle Centered Leadership* (New York: Simon and Shuster, 1991).

3 James Redfield, *The Celestine Philosophy* (New York: Warner Books, 1993).

4 Jack Canfield and Mark Victor Hansen, *Chicken Soup for the Soul* (and various other chicken soup titles) (Health Communications Inc., Deerfield Beach, Florida, 1996).

5 Lance H.K. Secretan, *Reclaiming Higher Ground* (Toronto: MacMillan Canada, 1997).

6 Stephen Covey, *The 7 Habits of Highly Effective People* (New York: Simon and Schuster, 1989).

7 James Collins and Jerry Porras, *Built to Last: Successful Habits of Visionary Companies* (New York: HarperBusiness, 1994).

8 C. William Pollard, *The Soul of the Firm* (New York: HarperBusiness, 1996).

COMMUNICATION

1 James D. Thompson, *Organizations in Action: Social Science Bases of Administrative Theory* (New York: McGraw Hill, 1967).

TRUST

1 Roger Fisher and William Ury, *Getting To Yes, Negotiating Agreement Without Giving In* (New York: Penguin, 1991).
2 Mary Rowe (MIT) "Workplace Intervention Techniques." Paper delivered at National Symposium on Conflict Resolution and Harassment in the Workplace. Hull, Quebec, October 1997.
3 Cathy Costantino, *Designing Conflict Management Systems: A Guide to Creating Productive and Healthy Organizations* (San Francisco: Jassey-Bass, 1996).
4 Gordon Shea, "Building Trust in the Workplace," American Management Association Monograph, 1984.
5 Peter Senge, *The Fifth Discipline, The Art and Practice of the Learning Organization* (New York: Doubleday, 1990).
6 Chris Argyris and Donald Schon, *Organizational Learning: A Theory of Action Perspective* (Reading MA: Addison-Wesley, 1978).
7 Jac Fitz-Eng, Saratoga Institute
8 Ralph Heintzman, "Continuous Learning," Report for the Canadian Centre for Management Development, Ottawa, 1994.

MANAGEMENT TOOLS

1 Richard Tanner Pascale, *Managing on the Edge: How Successful Companies Use Conflict to Stay Ahead* (New York: Penguin, 1990).
2 Eileen Shapiro, *Fad Surfing in the Boardroom: Reclaiming the Courage to Manage in an Age of Instant Answers* (Reading MA: Addison-Wesley, 1995), p. xiii.
3 Michael Hammer and James Champy, *Reengineering the Corporation: A Manifesto for Business Revolution* (New York: HarperBusiness, 1993).
4 Ole Ingstrup, *Reengineering in the Public Service: Promise or Peril* (Ottawa: Canadian Centre for Management Development, 1995).

4 Jac Fitz-Eng, Saratoga Institute
5 Christopher Pollitt, "Managerialism Revisited." In Guy Peters and Donald Savoie, eds, *Taking Stock, Assessing Public Sector Reforms,* 45–77 (Montreal: McGill-Queen's University Press, 1998).

TEAMWORK

1 Warren Bennis and Patricia Ward Biederman, *Organizing Genius: The Secrets of Creative Collaboration* (Reading, MA: Addison-Wesley, 1997).
2 Ibid., pp. 1,5,199
3 *Profit Magazine* (June 1997): 66.
4 Jon Katzenbach and Douglas K. Smith, *The Wisdom of Teams: Creating the High Performance Organization* (Cambridge, MA: Harvard Business School, 1993).
5 Peter Senge, *The Fifth Discipline: The Art and Practice of the Learning Organization* (New York: Doubleday, 1990).
6 Siobhan Alderson, in *Personnel Review* 22, no. 6 (1993): 53–62.
7 Edward De Bono, *Six Thinking Hats* (Toronto: Key Porter, 1985).

CHANGE MANAGEMENT

1 Barbara Moses, *Career Intelligence: Mastering the New Work and Personal Realities* (Toronto: Stoddart, 1997).
2 John Kotter, *Leading Change* (Cambridge, MA: HarvardBusiness School Press, 1996).
3 Richard Hooker, *Oxford Dictionary of Quotations* (Oxford: Oxford University Press, 1979), 255.

FINAL THOUGHTS

1 From A.A. Milne, *Winnie-the-Pooh*, illustration by E.H. Shepard. Copyright 1926 by E.P. Dutton, renewed 1954 by A.A. Milne. Used by permission of Dutton Children's Books, a division of Penguin Putnam Inc.
2 Herbert Simon, keynote address, Annual Conference of the American Society for Public Adminstration, July 1977, Philadelphia, PA.
3 Henry Mintzberg, in "Managing Government, Governing Management," *Harvard Business Review* (May/June 1996), makes a similar point.

4 James Collins and Jerry Porras, *Built to Last: Successful Habits of Visionary Companies* (New York: HarperBusiness, 1994).
5 C.William Pollard, *The Soul of the Firm* (New York: HarperBusiness, 1996).
6 James Redfield, *The Celestine Prophecy* (New York: Warner Books, 1993).
7 James Redfield, *The Tenth Insight* (New York: Warner Books, 1996).
8 Graeme Hodge and E.W. Russell, *"Privatization and Performance: International Indicators."* Paper presented to the American Society for Public Administration, Philadelphia, July 1997.
9 Lance H.K. Secretan, *Reclaiming Higher Ground* (Toronto: MacMillan Canada, 1997).
10 Charles L. Wallis, ed., *Words of Life* (New York: Harper and Row, 1966).

APPENDIX D

1 Lawrence E. Lynn Jr, *Public Management as Art, Science, and Profession* (Chatham, NJ: Chatham House, 1996).
2 John Kotter, *Leading Change* (Cambridge, MA: Harvard Business School Press, 1966), p. 100.
3 Thomas J. Peters and Robert H. Waterman, Jr., *In Search of Excellence* (New York: Harper and Row, 1982).
4 A critique of the study is found in "Who's Excellent Now," *BusinessWeek*, November 5, 1985, pp. 76–88.
5 James Collins and Jerry Porras, *Built to Last: Successful Habits of Visionary Companies* (New York: HarperBusiness, 1994).

Index

About the Authors

OLE MICHAELSEN INGSTRUP is the Commissioner of the Correctional Service of Canada. Born in Denmark, he received a masters in law and a doctorate in law from Aarhus University. He was a prison warden in Denmark and a representative on the European Committee on Crime Problems, the Council of Europe. In 1983 he emigrated to Canada, where he has served as chairman of the National Parole Board, principal of the Canadian Centre for Management Development, and senior advisor to the Privy Council Office. He has taught at the Far East Institute for the Prevention of Crime and Treatment of Offenders in Japan, Aarhus University, and was a Skelton-Clark Fellow at Queen's University Kingston. He was responsible for the promotion of public service renewal in the Canadian Federal Government under PS 2000. He is a governor of Carleton University.

His work has been recognized through his being made a knight and later a commander of the Order of the Dannebrog by the queen of Denmark; being made an honourary chief, Chief Spotted Eagle, by the Samson Cree for his work with aboriginal corrections; being recognized for leadership in corrections by the Volunteers of America Maude Booth Award.

He has authored several publications on law, corrections, and public service management, including *Reengineering in the Public Service, Promise or Peril*; *Public Service Renewal, from Means to Ends*; *Only Those Who Believe Can Stay The Course In Turbulent Times*; *Prisoners' Legal Rights*; *Structural Change in Prison Management; and Essays in Criminal Law*. He was responsible for the publication of *Our Story*, a case history of the transformation of the Correctional Service of Canada.

PAUL CROOKALL is a Canadian who obtained his masters of Business Administration and doctorate from the Ivey School of Business at the University of Western Ontario. He is a management consultant in private practice, specializing in corrections, public sector reform, health care, and crisis management. For 27 years he served with the Correctional Service of Canada, where he was senior advisor to the commissioner, executive director of the Regional Treatment Centre (Ontario), researcher, and internal management consultant.

He has taught management at Queen's University, Algonguin College, and the Correctional Staff College. He has consulted and studied in the Commonwealth, and presented papers at a variety of international gatherings. He is a certified health executive with the Canadian College of Health Service Executives, and a consultant with the Commonwealth Secretariat. He has been a member of the Senate and Board of Governors of the University of Western Ontario. He has received the Governor General's Exemplary Service Medal, and the American Correctional Association's Award for dedication to excellence in the field of corrections.